EARLY CAREER TEACHER ENTITLEMENT
GREAT EXPECTATIONS

TANYA OVENDEN-HOPE
AND HOLLY KIRKPATRICK

Together we unlock every learner's unique potential

At Hachette Learning (formerly Hodder Education), there's one thing we're certain about. No two students learn the same way. That's why our approach to teaching begins by recognising the needs of individuals first.

Our mission is to allow every learner to fulfil their unique potential by empowering those who teach them. From our expert teaching and learning resources to our digital educational tools that make learning easier and more accessible for all, we provide solutions designed to maximise the impact of learning for every teacher, parent and student.

Aligned to our parent company, Hachette Livre, founded in 1826, we pride ourselves on being a learning solutions provider with a global footprint.

www.hachettelearning.com

Although every effort has been made to ensure that website addresses are correct at time of going to press, Hachette Learning cannot be held responsible for the content of any website mentioned in this book. It is sometimes possible to find a relocated web page by typing in the address of the home page for a website in the URL window of your browser.

Hachette UK's policy is to use papers that are natural, renewable and recyclable products and made from wood grown in well-managed forests and other controlled sources. The logging and manufacturing processes are expected to conform to the environmental regulations of the country of origin.

To order, please visit www.HachetteLearning.com or contact Customer Service at education@hachette.co.uk / +44 (0)1235 827827.

ISBN: 978 1 0360 0682 2

© Tanya Ovenden-Hope and Holly Kirkpatrick 2025

First published in 2025 by
Hachette Learning (a trading division of Hodder & Stoughton Limited),
An Hachette UK Company
Carmelite House
50 Victoria Embankment
London EC4Y 0DZ

www.HachetteLearning.com

The authorised representative in the EEA is Hachette Ireland, 8 Castlecourt Centre, Dublin 15, D15 XTP3, Ireland (email: info@hbgi.ie)

Impression number   10 9 8 7 6 5 4 3 2 1
Year   2029 2028 2027 2026 2025

All rights reserved. Apart from any use permitted under UK copyright law, no part of this publication may be reproduced or transmitted in any form or by any means, electronic or mechanical, including photocopying and recording, or held within any information storage and retrieval system, without permission in writing from the publisher or under licence from the Copyright Licensing Agency Limited. Further details of such licences (for reprographic reproduction) may be obtained from the Copyright Licensing Agency Limited, www.cla.co.uk

Typeset in the UK.
Printed and bound by CPI Group (UK) Ltd, Croydon, CR0 4YY

A catalogue record for this title is available from the British Library.

MIX
Paper | Supporting responsible forestry
FSC™ C104740

REVIEWS

This book is an essential read for leaders involved in teacher development at both a school and system level, and particularly relevant at a time of crisis in teacher and leadership recruitment and retention. Tanya and Holly's work provides a clear and accessible guide to the development of the Early Career Framework together with a deep insight into the impact of years of educational reform in England. It is a timely reflection on how compliance to a framework is not helping teachers to gain the nuance and professional skills to be great classroom practitioners, and presents a compelling case not only for greater depth and support during their early career but for a career-long entitlement to professional development. At a time when far too many early career teachers leave within the first two years of the profession, we need a significant investment in a development programme that not only focuses on classroom techniques but recognises that teaching is about relationships and is as much an art form as a checklist of skills and knowledge in the current ECF.

Johanne Clifton, Director of Curriculum and Development, The Elliot Foundation Academies Trust, Hon Research Fellow, University of Birmingham

In this entertaining, informative and timely book the authors offer their own cautionary tale of the false comfort of uniformity and control. Through a thorough reflection on existing information and presentation of new research, they set out the opportunities to take a fresh look at the 'golden thread' to ensure we create a system of professional development for teachers and school leaders that is curious, collaborative and supports agency. Policymakers should take heed.

Gareth Conyard, CEO, Teacher Development Trust

This important new book on the ECF highlights its developments over the first few years of its implementation. We can never go backwards in education policy, only forwards – slowly amending the frameworks that we are given to make them into what are needed on the ground. This text helps us to examine the sense-making in this area of policy, and will be of interest to students and system stakeholders alike.

Dr Deb Outhwaite, Teacher Educator and Chair of BELMAS

A fascinating journey through the policy and practice associated with support and development for early career teachers in England. This book presents a lively, accessible and evidence-informed account of the current challenges facing early career teachers – and the wider teacher workforce – alongside an in-depth exploration of the policy interventions designed to tackle these issues. Combining both a critical and hopeful stance, the authors present a compelling case for further investment in and action for early career teachers and the systems designed to support them. Underpinned by a wealth of academic and professional experience and expertise, alongside the perspectives and voices of teachers, mentors and induction tutors, this book will be an invaluable resource for researchers, practitioners, policymakers and students working in this field.

Dr Rebecca Morris, University of Warwick

Professor Dr Tanya Ovenden-Hope is Dean of Place and Social Purpose and Professor of Education at Plymouth Marjon University. Tanya holds the highest professional status for teaching and learning in all three education sectors: school (FCCT), further education (FSET) and higher education (PFHEA). Her research on place-based inequity for schools, teacher supply and professional development has influenced thinking on the way schools access resources. She holds elected and invited roles for the British Educational Research Association (elected council member), International Council in Education for Teaching (vice-president, Europe) and the Paul Hamlyn Foundation Teacher Development Fund (advisory board member). Tanya is committed to teacher development and entitlement, and has led interventions and research to enhance and inform teacher professional learning.

Holly Kirkpatrick is head of Physical Education Teacher Training at the University of Buckingham. Her role includes training PE teachers and leading on a popular master's in sport programme. She has more than 13 years of teaching experience, in both state and independent sectors, as a PE teacher and director of sport. Holly is in the final stages of completing her educational doctorate, with a focus on the Early Career Framework. Her research interests include professional development and learning, and teacher recruitment and retention.

For Josef, Sammy and Oscar

Contents

Foreword by Rob Caudwell xiii

Introduction xvii

Chapter One: Hard Times: The teacher recruitment and
retention crisis 1

    Introduction 1

        Teacher recruitment 5

        Teacher retention 6

    Teacher experience case study 8

    The status of teaching 9

        What is 'status' and why is it important to teacher supply? .. 10

    Conclusion 15

    Teacher experience case study 17

Chapter Two: Bleak House: Unpicking the 'golden thread' 21

    Introduction 21

    Spinning the 'golden thread of teacher development' 22

    Preparing for the 'golden thread of teacher development'? 23

    Sewing the 'golden thread of teacher development' 26

    'Golden thread' strategy and reforms 27

        Teacher Recruitment and Retention Strategy, 2019 27

        The Early Career Framework, 2019 31

    Teacher experience case study 36

    Conclusion: the last stitch of the golden thread 38

Chapter Three: Great Expectations: Frameworks for 'great teaching' 41

  Introduction 41

  What is 'great teaching'? 42

    'What makes great teaching?' 43

    Implications for the Early Career Framework from 'What makes great teaching?' 47

    The notion of 'quality' in teaching 49

    Measuring quality teaching 50

  Teacher experience case study 51

  A Core Content Framework (CCF) for 'great teachers'? 55

  An Early Career Framework (ECF) for 'great teachers'? 56

  National professional qualifications (NPQs) for 'great teachers'? 57

  The Initial Teacher Training and Early Career Framework (ITTECF) for 'great teachers'? 58

    Considerations and potential challenges 60

  Conclusion 61

Chapter Four: The Old Curiosity Shop: Teacher experiences of the ECF 63

  Introduction 63

  The research: why we listened to teachers' experiences 64

    Our research methodology 65

    Teachers' expectations and experiences of the ECF 66

    Early career teachers' experiences of the ECF 68

    Benefits of the ECF to ECTs 68

    Challenges of the ECF to ECTs 71

    Mentors' experiences of the ECF 76

  Benefits of the ECF to mentors 78

  Challenges of the ECF for mentors 82

  Induction tutors' experiences of the ECF 87

  Benefits of the ECF for induction tutors 89

  Challenges of the ECF for induction tutors 90

 Teacher experience case study 93

 Conclusion 97

Chapter Five: Our Mutual Friend: The Initial Teacher Training and Early Career Framework (ITTECF) 99

 Introduction 99

 Rebirth 100

 Regeneration 102

 Teacher experience case study 106

 Education 110

 Greed 114

 Conclusion 116

Conclusion: The Chimes 119

 Introduction 119

 Enhancing Early Career Teacher Entitlement 120

 Considerations for place-based equity and ECTE 121

 Components of an effective Early Career Teacher Entitlement: a model for the future 123

Afterword by Professor Sonia Blandford 131

Glossary 135

References 139

Index 157

Foreword
By Rob Caudwell

Towards the end of *Great Expectations*, the novel's protagonist, Pip, reflects on his love for one of the other characters (avoiding spoilers here!). He muses, 'if you can tell me that you will go through the world with me, you will surely make it a better world for me, and me a better man for it, and I will try hard to make it a better world for you' (Dickens, 1861, p. 261). Pip's hope is for a loving companionship based on a long-term, two-sided commitment: that each party will at least try to make the world better for the other.

As we think about how best to guide new colleagues into the teaching profession, we are really talking about a similar two-sided commitment:

1. **What can we expect from and ask of early career teachers?** How are new teachers being prepared and equipped to make a positive, long-term impact in the classrooms and schools they are going into?

And:

2. **What can our new colleagues expect from and ask of us as a sector?** How are we best preparing the sector to welcome these new colleagues, so they feel cared for, supported and valued?

Early Career Teacher Entitlement: Great Expectations is an exploration of both halves of this relationship. As a sector, we want to benefit from wonderful new teachers coming into the profession. Education is far too important to not put considerable effort into helping every new teacher become brilliant at their new job, but the sector needs to offer wonderful careers to every new teacher too. There are obvious ethical reasons to seek to provide excellent employment to our newest colleagues, but there are also pragmatic ones: if we don't, they may well simply leave! We need to enable this long-term, two-sided commitment between new teachers and their chosen sector. We hope to make a better world for them, and them for us.

In this important book, Tanya Ovenden-Hope and Holly Kirkpatrick show that legislating for long-term, mutually beneficial early career provision at a national level has proven far from easy! Over the past few years, successive Conservative and now Labour governments have invested a huge amount of time, effort and money in revising and reforming how the sector welcomes new teachers into the profession – with the next round of reviews planned for 2027. As we consider the policy changes that have already happened, and further reforms that may come, we must keep these questions of a two-sided commitment in mind: *Are we succeeding in supporting new teachers to positively impact the teaching world? Are we succeeding in making the teaching world a better place for these new teachers?*

This book unpacks some of the progress that has been made, as well as some of the opportunities that seem to have been missed. Drawing on extensive expertise, evidence and experience – including their own primary research – Tanya and Holly thoroughly explore both the benefits and challenges that the various national approaches have encountered over the past few years. Pulling together emerging themes, they offer encouragement that some real, identifiable progress has been made in how the sector inducts early career teachers into the profession. Alongside this, they identify where there may have been mistakes and shortcomings – both in the efforts to prepare early career teachers for their careers in teaching, and in efforts to prepare the sector to support and welcome these new colleagues well.

Alongside their own expert analysis, Tanya and Holly have woven through this book the voices and stories of early career teachers, their mentors and their induction tutors. This is so important. This is a book underpinned by the first-hand experiences of those who have recently joined the teaching profession and those who have been helping to welcome these new teachers into our sector. Many of these stories are truly inspirational, as in them you will read about the wonderful commitment and professionalism that early career teachers and those supporting them are showing to one another and to their work. But these stories are also often sobering. They are important reminders that it is possible for policy and implementation decisions to have significant negative impacts for the very people these initiatives were designed to help. We must listen to these accounts carefully.

The book culminates in a fantastic set of recommendations for how best to build on these successes while addressing the challenges the sector is still facing. As the government moves towards its next review of the Early

Career Framework (ECF) in 2027, these recommendations offer a clear, comprehensive alternative to how early career teachers are currently being developed and supported. If we agree that our ultimate aim is to foster a two-sided commitment between early career teachers and their chosen sector – to make the world better for each other – Tanya and Holly's 'model for the future' offers a bold, exciting vision for what this could look like.

Rob Caudwell, former teacher, school leader and teacher educator, and co-founder of Penrose Education

Introduction

It has always been my opinion since I first possessed such a thing as an opinion, that the man who knows only one subject is next tiresome to the man who knows no subject. Therefore, in the course of my life I have taught myself whatever I could, and although I am not an educated man, I am able, I am thankful to say, to have an intelligent interest in most things.

Charles Dickens, *The Wreck of the Golden Mary* (1898, p. 3)

Charles Dickens (1812–1870), the Victorian novelist, journalist, speaker and social critic, experienced a childhood of hardship, as his father was imprisoned for debt and Dickens was sent to work at 12 years old in a boot-blacking factory to help support the family. Dickens's work demonstrates his belief that education had the potential to break the cycle of poverty but that he was sceptical of Victorian education's focus on the learning of facts alone. He used satire to challenge how children and adults outside of the ruling class were not encouraged to think about issues or life, but instead to accept what they were told were truths without explanation or consideration.

His Christmas story, *The Wreck of the Golden Mary* (1898), shines a light on Dickens's belief in the importance of self-development through the acquisition of knowledge and understanding, regardless of what the education system may support or allow. His portrayals of the Victorian education system as a controlled, and controlling, structure has prophetic echoes of the education system in contemporary England. This book explores the position of teacher development within an education landscape that is government controlled and standardised, with education reforms founded (and using) evidence approved by the bodies formed and funded by the government.

We suggest that opportunities within this education system for teachers' professional growth are present, but are bound by the 'facts' or evidence base that the government has approved as the best knowledge to develop practice. Beginning teachers 'don't know what they don't know', and standardisation of content, poor modelling in delivery and high workloads in the current teacher development frameworks, along with high accountability for student progress and outcomes being tied to teacher quality, do not encourage or support teacher enquiry into practice beyond that presented to them. In a recent edition of the Chartered College of Teaching's journal, *Impact*, the challenges of the current education landscape for the teaching profession were confirmed:

A combination of high workloads, insufficient support for early career teachers and the pervasive effect of policy reforms prioritising accountability over teacher wellbeing contributes to a challenging landscape for the teaching profession.

Lee (2025, p. 4)

It should therefore be no surprise that in England, where teaching has had its status as a profession undermined (Ovenden-Hope et al., 2022a), the recruitment and retention of teachers has been an ongoing challenge (Department for Education, 2022; Howson, 2020).

The years 2020 and 2021 saw the Covid-19 pandemic mask the crisis in teacher recruitment and retention in England, with England experiencing an increase in the number of trainee teachers, and fewer teachers leaving teaching, in response to fears and changes in the economy, and the perceived safety of a public-sector job (a typical response during periods of economic recession) (Hutchings, 2010). The increase in teachers joining and staying in teaching during the pandemic was not sustained when the pandemic ended (Worth & Faulkner, 2022). In 2022 one-fifth of teachers left the profession after two years (Education Support and Public First, 2023), representing a return to teacher attrition levels similar to those of 2018.

The Teacher Recruitment and Retention Strategy (Department for Education, 2019) had been introduced shortly before the Covid-19 pandemic and was the government's response to the sustained challenges in teacher supply in England. The strategy was operationalised during and after the pandemic through a range of reforms, and outlined four key areas where focus, investment and reform were considered to have the biggest impact on improving teacher recruitment and retention:

1. Create the right climate for leaders to establish supportive school cultures.

2. Transform support for early career teachers (ECTs).
3. Build a career offer that remains attractive to teachers as their careers and lives develop.
4. Make it easier for great people to become teachers.

Professional development was an attractive solution to teacher attrition, providing enhancement to knowledge and skills that could improve teacher self-efficacy, widely evidenced to support retention (Ovenden-Hope et al., 2020; Tzivinikou, 2015). The government's core reform from the strategy was for ECT development through a new Early Career Framework (ECF) of support and development, which it believed would change teaching in a way not seen for a generation:

At the centre of this strategy is the most significant reform to teaching in a generation – the introduction of the Early Career Framework (ECF).

Department for Education (2019, p. 6)

The government rolled out the ECF at pace (Ovenden-Hope, 2022), making it mandatory for all state-funded primary and secondary schools in England from September 2021. The challenges for schools in such a wide-sweeping reform becoming mandatory on the heels of the Covid-19 pandemic, and the issues for lead providers in developing the programmes, are discussed in our first book, *The Early Career Framework: Origins, Opportunities and Outcomes* (Ovenden-Hope, 2022).

The ECF became the first stitch of the government's 'golden thread of teacher development', coming after ITT and before national professional qualifications (NPQs), both of which were also reformed as part of the Teacher Retention and Recruitment Strategy, to support the government's plan for a standardised and connected route for teachers' professional development (Universities' Council for the Education of Teachers (UCET), 2022). The ECF was government funded and extended Early Career Teacher Entitlement (ECTE), but was not offered to ECTs in independent schools, early years or further education (post-16 colleges).

The ECF enhanced entitlement for beginning teachers was:

1. a two-year induction period
2. a 10% timetable reduction in the first year and a 5% reduction in the second year
3. mentoring support throughout the two-year induction period

4. professional development based on a programme approved for the ECF.

The ECTE provided by the ECF recognised that teachers' professional growth increases rapidly in their first few years, and that initial teacher training (ITT) programmes cannot cover everything a new teacher needs to know (Plymouth Marjon University, 2021). The enhanced ECTE of the ECF was welcomed by the education sector, the possibility of funded, high-quality CPD having been missing from England's schools for too long. The funded revised NPQs were also welcomed by school leaders, and offered a suggestion that the government had considered the benefits of career-long entitlement to the teaching profession.

In 2021, the Education Endowment Foundation (EEF) – an education charity established with government funding to develop research evidence for school improvement, particularly for schools with high levels of disadvantaged students – published a guidance report on effective professional development for teachers (Education Endowment Foundation, 2021). It is interesting to reflect on the disconnect between the EEF's recommendations and the ECF, particularly considering the EEF was involved in the development of the ECF and charged with the task of approving all evidence for teacher development used in the ECF (and CCF and NPQs).

The EEF guidance report (Education Endowment Foundation, 2021) recommended a mechanism-based approach to professional development, with greater flexibility and potential for teaching transformation. The report identified four categories for effective professional development – Build Knowledge, Motivate Staff, Develop Teaching Techniques, Embed Practice – all emphasising the underlying mechanisms that make professional development effective, rather than prescribing specific content or approaches as in the ECF. It highlights the importance of not just delivering content but also ensuring it is implemented and sustained, with all four categories working together to transform teaching.

It is interesting to note, however, that the Build Knowledge category of the EEF report (Education Endowment Foundation, 2021) includes managing cognitive load and revisiting prior learning, advocating a cognitive science perspective as the best approach. Cognitive science has been the underpinning approach in teacher development reform since 2019, articulated clearly in the ECF, CCF and NPQs, and a cause for concern if used without reference to the full range of perspectives and approaches supporting teaching and learning that could be used to inform teachers' choices for most effective classroom practice.

Had the government employed some of the mechanisms of the EEF report (Education Endowment Foundation, 2021) in the implementation of the ECF, it may not have received as much criticism so quickly (Ovenden-Hope, 2022b). It became clear from concerns raised by school leaders, ECTs and ECT mentors that there were aspects of this ECTE that warranted critical examination. The Department for Education (DfE) announced a review of the ECF (and of the ITT Core Content Framework, CCF) in 2023, in a call for evidence (Department for Education, 2023a) (although 'evidence' was challenging at this time given that the ECF had not run through a full phase). Findings from the review of the ECF (and CCF) led to further reform to teacher development, with a new framework combining the ITT CCF with the ECF – the ITTECF – announced by the DfE in January 2024. The ITTECF, designed to align trainee teacher and ECT training, development and support as a three-year programme, was implemented in all state-funded schools in September 2025 (Department for Education, 2024b).

In this book we explore the 'great expectations' of the ECF ECTE (and ponder career-long teacher entitlement) through the experiences of 50 teachers – ECTs, mentors and induction tutors – who participated in the first two-year cohort of the ECF (2021–2023), while also examining evidence from across the education sector on teacher development research, policy and reforms. We hope that the content of this book will provoke further consideration of what teachers' professional development is for, what makes it effective and whether the ITTECF (Department for Education, 2024b) is what the education system in England needs. The Labour government will review the ECF again in 2027, acknowledging that the ECTE needs more thought. We hope our book will help a little with its musings.

It has been nearly 200 years since Dickens wrote of the terrible social and working conditions of Victorian England, yet working conditions for teachers in England today have been blamed for teacher shortages. These conditions refer not only to lower pay than other professions but also to low status, poor autonomy and high accountability. The Recruitment and Retention Strategy (Department for Education, 2019) was supposed to offer a solution to teacher shortages, using the ECF and the 'golden thread of teacher development' to create better support for teachers throughout their careers, making it a more attractive profession. It has not worked.

Throughout this book we use teachers' voices, sharing lived experiences of the ECF, to illuminate our observations and provocations. Each chapter offers a 'teacher experience case study', while starting with a chapter title and quote taken from a Dickens novel, to position our considerations of teacher development in the shadow of a draconian era – a warning perhaps of what once was for education and what could be again given the path taken so far. As Dickens realised, the sharing of hard truths is often needed to effect change. *Bleak House* was a statement of support for the reform of the English and Welsh judicial system through the Judicature Acts in the 1870s.

The Labour government in England, elected in 2024 after years of Conservative rule, presents an opportunity to change the education landscape, fundamental to which is effective, process-driven ECTE. The crisis in teacher recruitment and retention can be mitigated if teaching – and teachers – are supported in being the free-thinking, agentic professionals that their students deserve through teacher development that is sustained and personalised. Raising awareness of the neoliberal, economistic ideology inherent in teacher development may provoke a different way of thinking about CPD for England's schools.

It is true that 'How Not To Do It' was the great study and object of all public departments and professional politicians.

Charles Dickens, *Little Dorrit* (1857, p. 58)

Reflecting, for **chapter one**, on Dickens's observations from *Hard Times* in 1854, it is clear that those in government controlling teaching wreaked havoc on education, establishing the 'teaching of facts' as the norm, to limit opportunities for students to think, and maintaining the societal status quo. This historical lens is useful when considering the current global crisis in teacher recruitment and retention, alongside the complex and ongoing teacher supply issues in England. We explore how ECTs are more likely than more experienced teachers to leave teaching, and the factors that contribute to teacher attrition, including high workload, and lack of autonomy and accountability.

We examine the ECF as a reform introduced to mitigate the crisis in teacher recruitment and retention, and consider whether it can ever achieve this aim as part of the ITTECF given the revisions made to the content and delivery from 2025. The chapter concludes with a consideration of the status of teaching, and the relationship of teacher and teaching status to teacher recruitment and retention in England. We question whether government control of teaching is the cause of a low-status teaching profession, and whether teaching can become a graduate career of choice through an enhanced ECTE.

Chapter two: Bleak House moves us to unpick the government's 'golden thread of teacher development' in an attempt to understand the origins for the spinning of this approach to CPD. We examine the Teacher Recruitment and Retention Strategy (Department for Education, 2019) and the ECF (Department for Education, 2019a) through evidence from reviews and research. Reflecting on standardisation within the ECTE, we remember the warning in Dickens's novel that, when education fails to recognise individuality, it allows only competency, not transformation.

The four commitments made in the Recruitment and Retention Strategy (Department for Education, 2019) are revisited in turn – for example, 'Is it easier for great people to become teachers?' – to understand if they have yet been met or could ever be met with the frameworks on offer. Reflecting on teacher entitlement as the last stitch for the 'golden thread', we wonder if the thread will lose its gilt if the professional development underpinning ECTE lacks the design, delivery and content for effective professional development.

The concepts used in government reform of teacher development are explored in **chapter three: Great Expectations**. We focus on the notion of professional development frameworks for 'great teachers'. What does the government mean by a 'great teacher'? What makes 'great teaching'? Where did the idea of 'great' in relation to teaching and teachers come from, and why is this important in relation to the CCF and ECF? We attempt to answer these questions by examining key reports that appear to have influenced government thinking, and show how they influence, or offer implications for, current teacher development reforms.

'Great teaching' is not fully understood, however, without exploring the notion of 'quality' in teaching and of teachers. Like 'great', 'quality' is a nebulous concept that is hard to define and becomes bound in ideology when measured. In teaching, quality becomes a proxy for effectiveness and this in turn is measured by student outcomes, which are at best an inaccurate indication of teacher or teaching quality, and at worst misrepresentative of it. To make this even more complicated, we do think that quality of teaching should be part of teachers' entitlements, but how it is defined, supported and measured is what requires deeper consideration by schools and policymakers. Chapter three concludes with a consideration of the CCF, ECF, NPQs and ITTECF as vehicles to develop and support 'great teachers' and a foundation for entitlement in teachers' professional development.

In **chapter four: The Old Curiosity Shop** we share our primary research exploring teachers' expectations and experiences of the ECF at the end of the first two-year programme in 2023. We interviewed 50 teachers – ECTs, mentors and induction tutors – in an attempt to understand how they engaged with the ECF and how this affected them in their role. We used what they told us to establish themes so that we could make sense of what they told us in relation to the ECF as a 'system' working in, with and for the wider education system.

The ECTs, mentors and induction tutors in our research reported both positive and negative experiences of the ECF. The positive experiences had enhanced their practice through new ideas, insights and relationships that had developed their self-confidence and self-efficacy as teachers and/or in their ECF role. The ECF had connected these teachers with other teachers, such as through classroom observations, or mentor–ECT meetings. These experiences met some of the great expectations held for the ECF by the ECTs, mentors and induction tutors. The poor experiences of the ECF, such as the prescribed, basic and generic content of materials that were delivered poorly and without context, and the additional time and work beyond the allowance given, were detrimental to the effectiveness of the framework for supporting teachers' growth and wellbeing.

Chapter five: Our Mutual Friend? uses the themes of Dickens's book to explore the government's teacher development reform, the Initial Teacher Training and Early Career Framework (ITTECF), currently in place for teachers at the beginning of their career in England. We take his themes of rebirth, regeneration, education and greed as a lens through which to examine the ITTECF. What are the origins of the ITTECF, from where has it been 'reborn'? Does the 'rebirth' of the new combined framework have a clear rationale for the changes put in place? Have similar models of teacher development in international settings been used to 'educate' and inform the new approach, with benefits and risks fully considered? Is there a 'greed' in the government reform, a hunger for control that undermines the key purpose of the ITTECF – to create effective teacher development in order to improve teacher recruitment and retention?

We argue that something has to be done to improve the culture of CPD in schools, as research shows that teachers in England have less engagement with professional development than in any other western country. This returns us to consideration of the neoliberal ideology within government reform of teacher training and education when examining issues of control and prescription in the ITTECF. We hope that insights on the ITTECF presented in this chapter may be useful for future revisions of ECTE and may also support a career-long entitlement for teachers in England.

Our **conclusion**, on teacher development and ECTE, comes with **The Chimes**, reflecting not only on what could have been but also what could be. We rehearse the possibilities for enhancing ECTE and suggest components for effective ECTE, based on the evidence presented in the previous chapters. We finish our book with a story, 'Great expectations of entitlement – a tale of teacher enrichment', having borrowed so much inspiration from Dickens for this work. In our story we imagine a future where teaching is a high-status profession, a result of radical reform in teacher entitlement. In this future Dickens's dream of an education system that develops enquiring minds is possible. We do, however, need to apologise to Dickens for our clumsy prose!

An Ode to the Early Career Teacher's Journey

In England's schools, a tale unfolds,
Of teachers new, with dreams untold.
A framework built, a golden thread,
To ease their steps, or feel like lead?

The Early Career Framework was put in place,
A change in focus at quite a pace.
Two years' support, with mentors near,
But many resources were not that clear.

Behaviour, pedagogy, curriculum too,
Assessment skills and what teachers do.
Not always landing when it should,
Sequence, context – knock on wood.

Yet challenges form where hopes reside,
As equity struggles still divide.
In schools where resources are stretched too thin,
The fight for fairness must begin.

Retention rates – a daunting fight,
With large percentages gone from sight.
The power of entitlement still resounds
But feels as if it's out of bounds.

And Labour dreams of what could be:
Personalised learning and agency.
Support for mentors, hours a plenty,
But not just yet, go gently, gently.

Questions linger in the air:
Will entitlement come? Does the government care?
For promises made in a manifesto,
Are hard to reform from the get-go.

So review is promised in a couple of years,
As the ITTECF gets into gear.
Trainees transition to ECTs,
On a golden thread designed for ease.

Standardised training that toes the line.
Contextually challenged, leaving mentors to find
The resources that ECTs really desire
To do their jobs well and keep out of the mire.

Chapter One
Hard Times: The teacher recruitment and retention crisis

Now, what I want is Facts. Teach these boys and girls nothing but Facts. Facts alone are wanted in life. Plant nothing else, and root out everything else.

Charles Dickens, *Hard Times* (1854, p. 13)

Introduction

In 1854 Dickens captured the essence of an educational philosophy in England that prioritised practical knowledge over any form of imagination or creativity. The warning that Dickens served, in his critique of an education system that neglects the development of critical thinking, empathy and emotional intelligence, appears almost prophetic in our post-Conservative education system. Facts are undoubtedly essential, but not in isolation or at the expense of a full and balanced education that promotes the skills needed to explore, understand, synthesise, adapt and use those facts in appropriate contexts. A government that extends this approach to teacher training, development and practice is at risk of creating 'hard times' for teacher recruitment and retention.

There is an international crisis in teacher recruitment and retention (Eurydice, 2021; Ovenden-Hope, 2021; Ovenden-Hope & Passy, 2020). Attracting and keeping enough teachers to meet school needs has for many years been challenging for, and challenged by, the agencies that control teacher supply (See, 2022). The United Nations Educational, Scientific and Cultural Organization's (UNESCO) Sustainable Development Goal 4, launched in 2015 as part of the Education 2030 Framework for Action (UNESCO, 2015, p. 21), with the aim to 'ensure inclusive and equitable quality education and promote lifelong opportunities for all'. Target 4.c of SDG 4 called for a substantial 'increase [in] the supply of qualified teachers'. In England in 2023, 42.2% of teachers had left the profession by year ten, 25.9% by year three (Department for Education, 2024g). In the United States, then education secretary, Miguel Cardona, warned of disruptions caused by teacher shortages, with the National Education Association reporting that 55% of educators were ready to leave the profession in 2022 (Camera, 2022).

The cause of this international crisis in teacher supply, which has schools stuck in a cycle of struggling to recruit teachers to plug the gaps left by those that leave, is difficult to evidence (Ovenden-Hope, 2022a). There are few robust longitudinal studies exploring the reasons for teacher shortages (See et al., 2020), or solutions (See et al., 2020) to address the recruitment and retention problem. Governments attempt to support schools by focusing on financial packages to attract new teachers (especially in subjects perceived in the previous year to be falling short of required teacher numbers), while failing to secure the retention of experienced teachers (See, 2022).

Teacher recruitment and retention in England faces significant challenges, mirroring global trends. The DfE data on the school workforce in England at the end of 2023 (the most up-to-date data on the teacher workforce available at the time of writing) demonstrated that the key issues affecting teacher supply were recruitment, identifying that, 'teacher vacancies (full and part time) had more than doubled in the past three years; from 1,100 in November 2020 to 2,800 in November 2023', with a 25.9% attrition rate for teachers who had qualified three years before (Department for Education, 2024g). With recruitment falling short of targets and increased numbers of teachers leaving the profession, the teacher workforce in England has experienced a sustained, now critical, shortage (see Figure 1).

Falling recruitment and rising leaving rates point to the escalating severity of teacher under-supply in England.

McClean et al. (2024, p. 4)

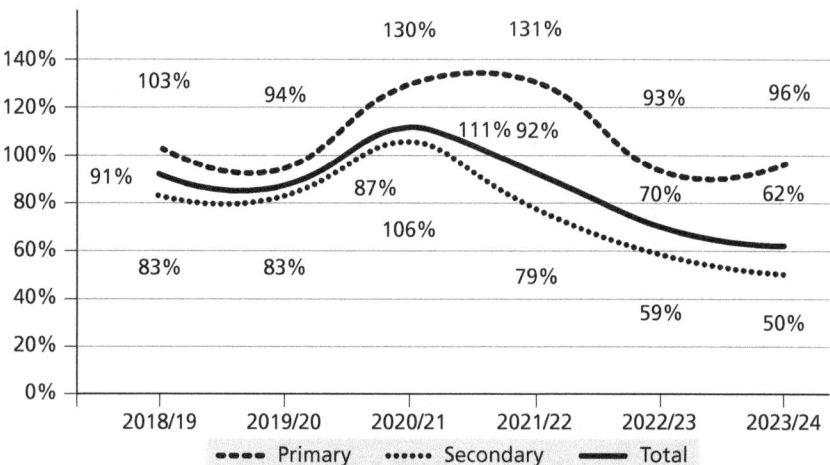

Figure 1: School workforce in England 2018/19–2023/24 Source: House of Commons (2024, p. 13)

The recruitment of trainee teachers did not achieve the government targets in 2023/24 for primary or secondary ITT, triggering calls for action from the government for fear of worsening teacher supply issues:

Recruitment to both primary and secondary ITT in 2023/24 was below the target number of trainees that the DfE estimated the school system needed to recruit to meet future staffing needs. This shows that post-pandemic teacher recruitment in England continues to be a significant policy challenge and is likely only to worsen without concerted action. Last year's under-recruitment was most severe for secondary, which only reached half of its target.

McClean et al. (2024, p. 10)

National data on the teacher labour market in England suggests that the supply of new trainees is insufficient to meet future demand for teachers in the classroom.

In England, the ECF was conceived by the government as core to its Teacher Retention and Recruitment Strategy (Department for Education, 2019) and part of a 'golden thread of teacher development' that would improve teacher retention (as well as potentially attract graduates to teaching). The leaving rate data for ECTs (teachers in their first two years of teaching) show that they are more likely to leave teaching than are more experienced teachers (Department for Education, 2024g). The School Workforce Census (2022/23) informs the DfE School Workforce in England reporting, which reports broadly similar leaving rates for first-year ECTs compared to all other teachers (Department for Education, 2024g).

Post-pandemic ECT attrition after one year of teaching in 2021/22 was at 1%, which was slightly lower than all other teacher attrition at 3% (Department for Education, 2024g). While the government may be quick to attribute this to the introduction of the ECF in September 2021, there could be many drivers responsible for this reduced comparable attrition of ECTs. One alternative explanation for this could be the targeted pay increases for ECTs that resulted in higher pay growth (McClean et al., 2024). ECT attrition remains high, currently standing at 11.3% after one year of teaching and 25.9% by year three of teaching (Department for Education, 2024g). The responsibility of the ECF to impact directly on ECT attrition was always going to be a formidable task because of the other variables acting on teacher recruitment and retention.

Early indicators from lead providers, school leaders and academics for improvements to the ECF to support ECT retention

In The Early Career Framework: Origins, Outcomes and Opportunities (Ovenden-Hope, 2022), written as the ECF was being introduced to schools in England, lead providers, school leaders and academics gave clear messages on the changes that needed to be made to the ECF timing for implementation, content and delivery. These messages referred to areas of the ECF that were seen to impact on ECT experience and thereby had the potential to retain ECTs. The key messages were:

- School context matters in CPD, and the ECF programme content and delivery should be adapted to align with this.

- Prior learning and knowledge of both ECTs and mentors matter, and the ECF programme content should be flexibly delivered to support this.

- Workload is important and the ECF programme should not add to this for ECTs or mentors in any way that is not supported by the time allocated by the school via DfE funding.

- National reform to existing school practices takes time, schools need to be able to plan for CPD against their priorities and put timetables in place to support new roles.

- Schools that choose to design and deliver their own ECF programme should have access to funding for training of ECTs and mentors, and free appropriate body services.

Source: Ovenden-Hope (2022, pp. 297–298)

Teacher recruitment

The recruitment of new teachers in England has become increasingly difficult, particularly in secondary schools. The National Foundation for Educational Research (NFER) reported that ITT recruitment for the 2024/25 academic year projected shortfalls to recruitment targets in all but three secondary subject areas (McClean et al., 2024). This trend is corroborated by the Teacher Tapp, Gatsby, and SchoolDash annual report, which revealed a 12% increase in job advertisements in 2024 compared to the previous year, with 13% of secondary teachers reporting unfilled vacancies within their subject departments (Allen et al., 2024).

Teacher recruitment remains particularly problematic for specific subjects in secondary schools. In 2023, physics teacher recruitment was 83% below target, while design & technology and modern foreign languages faced shortfalls of 73% and 67%, respectively (Maisuria et al., 2023). These figures represent a worrying and sustained trend, with the postgraduate teacher recruitment target having been met only once since 2015/16. What is additionally concerning are reports that GCSE science classes are being taught by non-specialist teachers in one-third of cases (Chong et al., 2024). This shortage of qualified teachers in specific subjects could have long-term implications for the quality of education in these areas (Ovenden-Hope et al., 2022).

It should also be recognised that unqualified teachers do not have entitlement to the support of the ECF, as the ECF forms part of the induction for teachers who hold QTS. The increasing reliance of schools on the use of unqualified teachers on temporary contracts to cover unfilled posts has become a necessity due to the difficulties identified above with teacher recruitment (Ovenden-Hope, 2023). For unqualified ECTs without ECF entitlement, their support is reliant on a school already struggling to recruit teachers, and therefore likely to be minimal. That said, the loss of an unqualified ECT on a temporary contract does not show in DfE workforce data and as such is not an easily identifiable concern for teacher retention. However, if the mission of the government is to have 'great teachers' (see chapter three), deregulation and the use of unqualified ECTs with no formal support should be a primary concern, not only for teacher retention but also for the quality of teaching and learning.

The government in England articulated what it believed all new teachers should know, and be able to do, through the ECF (Department for Education, 2019a). This belief has not changed with the ITTECF implemented in September 2025 (Department for Education, 2024b). Content is prescriptive, underpinned by evidence referenced in the ECF (Department for Education, 2019b) and aligns with the 'golden thread' of teacher development mapped by the DfE from the Initial Teacher Training Core Content Framework to the national professional qualifications (see chapter two for more on the 'golden thread of teacher development').

Teacher retention

The retention of teachers, and ECTs specifically, is as concerning as the recruitment of teachers in maintaining teacher supply in England. Retaining ECTs has been an ongoing challenge, with current retention data demonstrating that the problem is not going away. The research exploring the factors that cause ECT attrition reports a complex picture and suggests that, regardless of the quality of support and training provided by the ECF, ECTs are likely to continue leaving in numbers high enough to negatively affect supply.

The National Association of Schoolmasters Union of Women Teachers (NASUWT) found that the main reasons for teacher and school leader dissatisfaction were high workload, pupil behaviour, budget cuts, pay and accountability (NASUWT, 2019). However, there is also contradictory evidence that ECTs are 'not primarily motivated to leave the profession by the prospect of increased pay' (Worth et al., 2018, p. 5). It has also been argued that ECTs primarily go into the profession to make a difference, and leave when teaching does not meet this expectation (Menzies, 2019).

Factors contributing to the teacher retention crisis

Workload and work–life balance

High workload consistently emerges as a primary factor driving teachers away from the profession. The Teaching and Learning International Survey (TALIS) found that 53% of primary and 57% of secondary school teachers felt their workload was unmanageable. This issue has been further compounded by increased pressures since the Covid-19 pandemic.

Career progression and leadership

There is no career progression consideration in the ECF; when offered, this has been shown to support ECT retention. There is a growing reluctance among senior leaders to pursue headteacher positions, with only 43% aspiring to such roles, down from 56% pre-pandemic. This decline in leadership aspirations could lead to a shortage of experienced school leaders in the future.

Subject-specific challenges

Science departments in particular are struggling, with one in three science teachers reporting that non-specialist teachers were teaching GCSE science classes. This not only affects the quality of education but also potentially discourages students from pursuing these subjects further.

Source: Allen et al. (2024); Department for Education (2024f); Maisuria et al. (2023); McClean et al. (2024); Ovenden-Hope et al. (2020)

There is therefore a range of reasons for ECTs (and additional reasons for school leaders) leaving teaching. For ECTs, support for coping with the unexpected demands of teaching is crucial for retaining them in the profession (Ovenden-Hope et al., 2020). In an ideal teacher development world – one without neoliberal central government control, education marketisation and accountability (Ovenden-Hope & Kirkpatrick, 2025) – the ECF could make this ECT support possible. The mentoring of ECTs that underpins the ECF should allow mentors to provide clear guidance and strategies to ECTs in how to manage being a teacher in an increasingly demanding environment. The challenge in achieving this mentoring need is in the time given to mentors for their role, the training they receive to do the role and the capacity they have for support beyond the structure of the ECF programme content (see chapter four for further information on mentor experiences of the ECF).

Teacher experience case study

Early Career Teacher: left teaching in year two of the ECF

I found managing behaviour super hard throughout the ECF, even while teaching maths to my top sets. The pupils would get off task easily if I were not constantly watching them. For me, it was hard as a new teacher when pupils lacked effort, and I really struggled with that.

I enjoyed the termly meetings for the ECF programme with other ECTs, and in school we had an hour of CPD and discussion. I did the readings; however I don't feel that the ECF had a big impact on my teaching. I had a weekly meeting with my mentor, who I felt was supportive, and we discussed aspects of my teaching that I needed to improve, and how to develop behaviour strategies. I really liked observing other colleagues and learned a lot from that. I disliked teachers coming to observe my lesson for 10 minutes and then disappearing. The feedback I received from these observations was not effective. Observations need to happen with the same class so that progress can be seen and observers are aware of the context. My mentor was a head of department and we had a good relationship, however he was so busy at times I felt like an additional burden.

To be honest, the ECF is a blur. I remember some content on behaviour and managing classes, but it is impossible to remember everything. My teaching suffered when the behaviour of the pupils was poor, making a well-planned and organised lesson seem pointless. I had structures and plans in place for my lesson, but it didn't always go to plan. I felt

> unable to apply any of the content of the ECF as I tried just to get through the lessons. In school every day is hectic, and I struggled with the pace.
>
> I thrive on support and liked the support of my mentor when they could give it. However, I didn't like the online training or meetings, and was so tired by the end of the school day it was hard to find the motivation to attend. I preferred when we were off-site for the day attending training. When I was off teaching I could focus properly on the framework and not be distracted by teaching or tiredness. I had so many meetings and so much coaching I felt overwhelmed by it all.
>
> Teaching is hard. The pace of the school day meant I hardly got a break. Adding the ECF, this is where my feelings of being overwhelmed and stressed occurred. If I am honest, it was the added stress of the ECF that made me question being in teaching. I started teaching as an unqualified teacher in an independent school with small classes. I completed year one of the ECF in a state school with 32 students in each class. This was really tough, the pupils were challenging and needy, and as a teacher I had too many things to deal with.
>
> I started the ECF with lots of energy and wanted to help all the pupils, but even with my most able classes there were issues with neediness. It added to my tiredness and made me question my ability to teach. In year one of the ECF I struggled to see changes in my practice and was hesitant in speaking with my mentor as he was a head of department. Should I have been more honest or waited until I felt more secure? I decided to leave teaching in my second year of teaching in state school as I felt trapped and overwhelmed.

The status of teaching

Government recognition of the importance of professional development to an occupation is core to its professional status (Ovenden-Hope, 2022a). The ECF provides funded, structured professional development, which should offer official affirmation of the professional status of teaching and establish greater potential to attract more graduates towards teaching. However, the status of teaching has experienced sustained and systemic undermining, which leaves its position as a 'profession' under question, and recruitment and retention in crisis (Ovenden-Hope, 2022a).

What is 'status' and why is it important to teacher supply?

Status can be experienced both occupationally (through a job) and individually (through personal attributes), and both can be further experienced through an objective state – for example, how society perceives teaching or teachers – or subjectively – for example, how the individual feels about being a teacher. Status is therefore complex, and researchers have attempted to show how occupational status in teaching is different to prestige or esteem (Hoyle, 2001), in an attempt to categorise objective experiences of status. However, to understand how status could affect teacher recruitment and retention, it is important to define what status means in this context.

The word 'status' has a Latin origin, meaning 'standing' (Hargreaves & Flutter, 2013), and this meaning has been adapted in its common use as a noun to be understood as the 'respect and importance given to someone or something' (*Cambridge Dictionary*, 2022). Therefore, status has meaning in relation to both teaching (the way it is experienced by the profession as an occupation) and teachers (the way it is experienced by the individual teacher). The International Labour Organization (ILO) and UNESCO in 1966 recommended teachers' status be aligned with other professions:

The expression 'status' as used in relation to teachers means both the standing or regard accorded them, as evidenced by the level of appreciation of the importance of their function and of their competence in performing it, and the working conditions, remuneration and other material benefits accorded them relative to other professional groups.

ILO/UNESCO (2016, p. 21)

The ILO/UNESCO definition of status applies an objective meaning to status, but does not engage with the subjective experience of status that teachers have and that may affect their decision to remain or leave teaching. Therefore, while the nuanced approach to status that considers prestige and esteem is worth noting, understanding the full role of status in the teacher supply crisis requires focus on objective and subjective status, or teaching as a profession and teacher as professional. In a 2022 paper theorising teacher status, Ovenden-Hope defined status for teaching and teachers as follows:

Status is used in relation to teaching as an occupation, and teachers as individuals, and means respectively the level of regard and entitlements objectively given to the occupation by the public and other professions, and the subjective level of esteem given to the occupation by an individual.

Ovenden-Hope (2022a, p. 38)

The complexity in the establishment of teacher status is compounded by the fluidity between objective and subjective contextual issues – for example, teacher pay, which is established by policymakers, operationalised by schools, experienced by teachers and observed by the public, thereby flowing between the objective and subjective status domains of teaching and teachers. It is important to understand what status is in relation to teaching and teachers, in order to understand how it might contribute to teacher recruitment and retention. If status is about regard and entitlements, then, to flourish, teaching and teachers need to receive this in line with other professions.

Teaching as a profession

Status can only be understood with reference to teaching as a profession. Teaching requires specialist knowledge, training and skills (Ingersoll & Gregory, 2018), and should therefore have a status similar to that of other specialist careers, such as medicine. A profession, according to the dictionary, is 'respected because it involves a high level of education' (*Cambridge Dictionary*, 2025). Until 2012 teachers were graduates, regulated in their profession through qualified teacher status (QTS), but this professional identity has been 'marked by both confusion and contention' (Ingersoll & Gregory, 2018) because teaching has variable levels of training and increasing numbers of unqualified teachers due to the deregulation of teaching in 2012 by then secretary of state for education, Michael Gove (HM Government, 2012). Teachers in England lack control over their own terms and conditions (with agencies making decisions on issues on pay, conditions, quality and curriculum in other countries too) (Ovenden-Hope & Passy, 2020), and experience high accountability with a lack of autonomy (Worth & Van den Brande, 2020). For over a decade, researchers have concluded that teaching 'remains at best a semi-professional occupation' (Hargreaves & and Flutter, 2013), in England reduced and restricted by the control exerted over it by the government.

Measures of teaching and teachers' status

The status of teaching and teachers internationally, both objectively and subjectively, is low. In a report on global teacher status in 2018, teaching was ranked seventh out of 14 professions (Dolton et al., 2018), with no indication that this status has improved in recent years. The Covid-19 pandemic and worldwide lockdowns in 2020 created additional burdens on teachers to sustain hybrid models of virtual and face-to-face teaching, with little recognition at public level of the challenges being faced in doing this. At the height of the Covid-19 pandemic in 2020, the UK government briefly acknowledged the important role that schools, teaching and teachers played in supporting the world economy as 'a fundamental building block to national success' (Cordingley & Crisp, 2020, p. 146).

During the Covid-19 pandemic, the status of teaching and teachers was, very fleetingly, experienced objectively and subjectively as a higher-ranking profession. Schools were seen to support vulnerable children and those of key workers to engage in the economic and health-related activity needed to keep the world as we know it turning. However, the rise in status for teaching and teachers was short-lived, with media representation turning and subverting the work that schools and teachers were doing, reporting that schools were closed, and establishing a narrative that teachers were at home and assumed not to be teaching (Walters, 2022).

The government did nothing to stop this media representation of teachers and schools, and effectively undermined public regard for teachers and teaching. This was short-sighted of the government, as it was aware of teacher supply issues prior to the pandemic and should have realised that an erosion of the status of teaching and of teachers would affect the attractiveness of teaching as a career of choice – choice being the important word in a post-pandemic England with private-sector jobs offering greater flexibility in working conditions and higher pay for graduates. The status of teaching and teachers is directly affected by politics and educational policy, which in England has demonstrated neoliberal ideologies of increasing accountability, for example school inspection, and league tables of school and student performance, which reduce teacher and school autonomy in the name of raising standards and outcomes. Is a profession without autonomy a profession at all? If we reconsider the definition of status for teaching, it becomes clear that 'the level of regard and entitlements objectively given to the occupation' is low. The status of teaching and teachers as profession and professionals is low. This status will affect the choice of teaching as a 'profession' for graduates in England.

The control of teaching by central government agencies has contributed to a status-based crisis of teacher shortages by enabling a perception of teaching to become established in society and in individuals (habitus) that teaching is low status, so much so that the profession itself cannot be trusted to determine its own pay, conditions or curriculum, reinforced by low pay relative to other professions and external scrutiny of inspections.

Ovenden-Hope (2022a, p. 39)

In England it has been reported that agencies controlling teacher education since the 1970s have 'not coped well with external circumstances that have affected teacher supply' (Howson, 2020). Changes to the desirability of teaching as a career for graduates, on increasing numbers of teachers leaving teaching, has elicited a response by the DfE to treat teachers as a 'commodity', rather than professionals (Ovenden-Hope, 2021). This market-driven ideology does not align with other higher-status professions, such as medicine and law. Teachers as commodity (or product) can be managed and delivered by a number of teachers trained and serviced through delivering a set curriculum in a certain way.

Sadly, this commodification of teaching is evidenced in the way the 'golden thread' was articulated through the reforms of the ECF and NPQs and continues into the ITTECF (see chapter two). Agencies have focused government policy on 'enough teachers to meet demand, to secure the product (teacher) and to provide the service (teaching)' (Ovenden-Hope, 2021, pp. 72–73). Unfortunately this focus also resulted in more unqualified teachers being recruited to schools, further supporting the demise of the status of teaching and teachers with high level training and skills that are expected of a profession (Ovenden-Hope & Passy, 2020).

The DfE has had to ensure that there are enough teachers in schools to teach all the students, but with sustained teacher supply issues this has led to the loss of constructs we understand to constitute a professional, such as having a qualification. In England in 2019, there were 25,078 unqualified teachers in state-funded schools (Department for Education, 2019c). The reporting on unqualified teachers in DfE teacher workforce reports has changed to teacher highest qualification, making more up-to-date figures hard to identify. If it is assumed that the latest workforce data reporting teachers' highest qualification as 'degree or higher' does not include a teaching qualification (as other criteria include Bachelor of Education, PGCE and other non-standard teaching qualifications), then the number of unqualified teachers increased to 442,291 in 2023/24 (Department for Education, 2024g).

> **The consequences of a low teaching status**
>
> In societies where teaching is not perceived or treated as a profession, and teaching and teachers have low status, there are clear outcomes that include:
> - low initial teacher trainee numbers
> - challenges for teacher recruitment
> - high teacher attrition
> - increased numbers of unqualified/unlicensed teachers (deregulation).
>
> Source: Ovenden-Hope (2022a)

In England, the Conservative government engaged with teaching as a service that 'can be done by any seemingly competent adult (commodity) without a teaching qualification and, in some cases, a degree'; this devalues teaching as a profession (Ovenden-Hope, 2021, p. 73). The Labour government has pledged that all new teachers will be qualified, which brings some hope of a move towards re-regulation of teaching. If teaching is not regulated, the low status of teaching and teachers will cause further widening in the status (and subsequent reward) gap between teaching and other comparable professions. This in turn will decrease further the attractiveness of teaching to those considering it as a career and to those already teaching, and teacher shortages will prevail (see Figure 2).

The low status of teaching as a profession, and of teachers, is embedded in common understanding (habitus), reinforced by media representations and individual expectations and experiences as they live their lives.

Ovenden-Hope (2022a, p. 40)

Chapter One: Hard Times

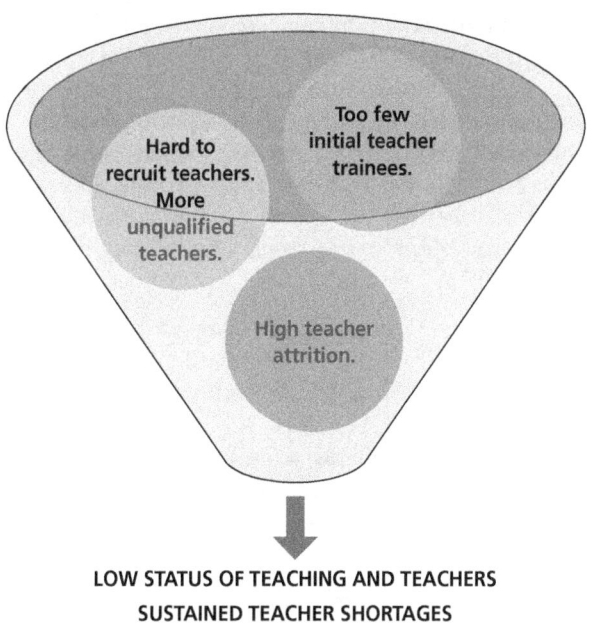

Figure 2: Status-based teacher shortages Source: Ovenden-Hope (2022a, p. 40)

Conclusion

The teacher recruitment and retention crisis in England shows no signs of abating, with both recruitment targets being missed and retention rates declining. Teaching can appear more attractive to postgraduates during economic downturns when other private-sector postgraduate careers are not available and graduate unemployment increases (Dolton et al., 2003). Teaching may well be considered 'recession proof', because the need for teachers remains, regardless of wider economic challenges (Hutchings, 2010). The challenge of this for teacher supply is that those entering teaching as a 'fallback' profession (Dolton et al., 2003) typically leave teaching as and when the economy recovers, and those who would have left teaching but stayed due to the pandemic, will also leave. This expectation of a double loss of teachers to the profession has played out in England, with high teacher attrition.

A demographic bulge of students entering secondary education (age 11) in 2025 will only add fuel to the teacher supply fire. The government belief that the ITTECF is the tool for extinguishing the flames of the recruitment and retention fire's development may be misplaced. A more holistic and systemic approach to solve decades of teacher supply issues (Howson, 2020) appears to be necessary. This should include ECT professional development, but also a more robust, career-long, funded system of context-relevant, personalised learning that develops their knowledge, understanding and skills for the career trajectory they decide they want to have. It is not a coincidence that the erosion of teacher status through education policy over the last decade has been matched by teacher shortages (Ovenden-Hope, 2022a).

Effective professional development in the first years of teaching can provide teachers with the self-efficacy needed to stay in the profession (Ovenden-Hope et al., 2020). Criticisms by education stakeholders of the ECF's poor contextualisation by ECT, school, subject and phase, and increased workloads for ECTs, mentors and schools, led to a review of the ECF by the DfE in 2023, and findings resulted in a new framework combining Initial Teacher Training and its Core Content Framework with the ECF (ITTECF).

The new ITTECF, mandatory in schools from September 2025, presents a national, sequenced curriculum of training and development for beginning teachers in England. As discussed in chapter five, it offers positive developments to areas of the ECF that impact on its effectiveness for ECT development. Whether this new ECT entitlement will affect ECT attrition, however, is yet to be seen. It is worth noting that the statutory requirements to deliver the ECF apply only if schools actually have an ECT. For schools already working at full capacity, challenged by the rising costs of running a school with no additional funding on the horizon, the additional demands on resources by the ECF can be avoided by not having an ECT. If schools avoid having ECTs, the crisis in teacher supply will become greater still.

Chapter One: Hard Times

Teacher experience case study

Mentor: Taz Hall

I am a head of a science faculty in a state secondary school and ECT mentor for the ECF. I have been a head of faculty for three years and was a key stage lead before that. I have been an ECT/NQT mentor for the past five years and have mentored for two different ECF programme providers. Mentor training wise, my previous school held meetings each term to discuss shared practice for mentors across the school. We also had termly mentor meetings with the provider. In my current school, training is more bespoke, based on the experience of the mentor. Observations of ECTs are done jointly with our ITT lead, and discussions regarding ECT progress are held termly. Training from this ECF provider is only once per year. ECTs in my faculty are mentored in teaching across the three sciences and for key stage 3 and 4 (11–16 age range). In my previous school I also mentored ECTs in teaching key stage 5 (16–18 age range).

I took on the role of ECT mentor as I wanted to make a positive contribution to the learning experience of children in other classrooms, not just my own. I believe that quality teaching should happen from the moment you step into a classroom, and I wanted to support other teachers in achieving their best practice through research-based pedagogy.

The current ECT framework has been varied in its rollout. And, from my perspective, ECT mentors within their local setting have 'muddled along' and made their own way. Provider PowerPoints and resources for both mentors and ECTs have been generic for each phase and do not encourage adaptive mentoring, or they react to the needs of the ECT at the time. Often videos have more information about the provider than palpable skills that ECTs can use!

I expected that the ECF providers would focus more on in-person training specific to the ECT. The generic 'watch this' videos, especially in the current recruitment climate, do nothing to support ECT engagement or retention. A poorly supported ECT will struggle in the profession and leave before their potential is realised. I have seen this

17

happen. Therefore to ensure my ECTs are well supported, I have relied more on my skills as a faculty lead to inform my mentoring than on any of the training given by the ECF provider.

Naively, I expected more time would be allocated by the DfE to support the ECTs as they undertook their ECF programme. After all, most of these teachers will only have had school experience through their initial teacher training placements. We expect these individuals to succeed with less time and development than a degree student. However, many of the ECTs I have encountered are individuals with indomitable spirit, tackling the profession as a vocation and giving as much as they can to develop in their role. I therefore feel it is our job as mentors to support, guide and protect our new teachers – to keep them in the profession and stop them from burning out by showing them how to balance the demands of the job.

Most school settings follow guidance from providers and the DfE, and allocate one hour a week in year one of the ECF to the mentoring of ECTs and one hour a fortnight in year two. This time allocation is nowhere near enough to support an ECT. Daily time for the mentor and ECT would be more appropriate. A mentor is needed to guide the ECT in every aspect of their pedagogy and practice. From how best to tackle any situation that may arise in the classroom, to helping them adapt their skills to the needs of each (very different) group they teach, to support with technology issues, finding resources to reduce their planning time and, if the ECT teaches a practical subject, then additional practical guidance is needed. Even if mentoring were to become just a welfare check-in with the ECT, this would need to happen on a daily basis.

In my faculty an ECT mentor will use two to three hours of their time to support their ECT each week, regardless of whether the ECT is in year one or two. This time typically increases the week before a holiday as ECTs are preparing for changes to their teaching when they return to school from the break. All ECTs need 'checking' support in the form of reassurances, such as being told, 'Yes you are brilliant and that's how I would tackle that situation.' Most mentors give up their time freely to support ECTs as they believe in the benefits of the role for the ECT.

> All this said, I would wholeheartedly recommend the role of ECT mentor to anyone willing to give up the time. Being a mentor is exceptionally fulfilling and most definitely 'worth it', especially when you see the individuals you have supported move on to greater successes as a teacher. Where things might become 'tricky' and 'less fulfilling' for a mentor is in supporting an ECT who is either struggling with the day-to-day expectations of teaching in a school (having believed the myth of 3pm finishes and long holidays), or an individual who is very self-reflective and can over-resource to the point of burnout. While this may be a generalisation, it has been raised within my faculty and discussed by the ECT mentors within my school setting.
>
> The reforms to the ECF will, I suspect, have no impact on my day-to-day mentoring. I have experienced frequent framework changes, and external providers offer more of a 'box tick' exercise that needs completing as an addition to the 'true' mentoring that we do in school. I would recommend that government officers spend time – not just fleeting visits, but extended time – 'at the chalk face' and speak with as many mentors as they can who have worked with ECTs that have remained in the profession. I have no doubt that they will find out that these mentors have given additional time through bespoke support to their ECTs, and it is this that has led to them deciding to stay in teaching.

Herein lay the spring of the mechanical art and mystery of educating the reason without stooping to the cultivation of the sentiments and affections. Never wonder. By means of addition, subtraction, multiplication, and division, settle everything somehow, and never wonder.

Charles Dickens, Hard Times (1854, pp. 56–57)

Chapter Two
Bleak House: Unpicking the 'golden thread'

He had been educated in no habits of application and concentration. The system which had addressed him in exactly the same manner as it had addressed hundreds of other boys, all varying in character and capacity, had enabled him to dash through his tasks, always with fair credit and often with distinction, but in a fitful, dazzling way that had confirmed his reliance on those very qualities in himself which it had been most desirable to direct and train.

Charles Dickens, *Bleak House* (1853, p. 265)

Introduction

Dickens's criticisms of the Victorian education system are writ large in *Bleak House* (1853), shining a light on the standardised practices in schools that fail to recognise individual differences, producing students who appear competent but lack the essential skills for sustained learning and critical thinking. Our question is, does the content of the 'golden thread of teacher development' do any better than this for our teachers?

Spinning the 'golden thread of teacher development'

The Conservative government in the United Kingdom (2010–2024) brought significant changes to the education landscape in England, including to teacher education and teachers' professional development (Ellis, 2024; Hordern et al., 2021). The reforms that have been implemented, intended to improve and enhance teacher development, reflect the government's managerial, marketised and performative neoliberal ideology (Ball, 2003). Education reform since 2010 has centralised power to the DfE for schools and teachers, which has eroded school and teacher autonomy (McIntyre et al., 2017). Policy claims for creating a schools-led system (HM Government, 2011) and government strategy being 'the start of a conversation with the profession' (Department for Education, 2019, p. 6) appear at odds with the education 'market' of standardised pedagogy, practice and managed performativity that its teachers experience (Ovenden-Hope & Kirkpatrick, 2025), not to mention a 'golden thread of teacher development'. It will be interesting to see if ECT teacher development escapes its neoliberal foundations under the Labour government for a more authentic teacher and schools-led offer of support.

The term 'golden thread' was first used by Dame Judith Hackitt in 2018, in the report 'Building a Safer Future' (Secretary of State for Housing, Communities and Local Government, 2018). While this report was not specifically relevant to an educational context it was used by the DfE, with the term 'golden thread' adopted by Justine Greening, then secretary of state for education, to explain a vision for teacher development. Justine Greening said that a 'golden thread' should be developed to 'empower new teachers with access to the sustained high-quality training and development that every professional needs' (Dickens, 2024).

The DfE formally incorporated a 'golden thread of teacher development' (Department for Education, 2019, p. 26) into the 2019 Teacher Recruitment and Retention Strategy (Department for Education, 2019). The Teacher Recruitment and Retention Strategy offered comprehensive reform for teacher development through four key commitments, all of which were intended to create a more cohesive, high-quality approach to teacher development, and ultimately make teaching a more attractive profession (more detail on the teacher recruitment and retention crisis in England can be found in chapter one).

> **Four key commitments in the Teacher Recruitment and Retention Strategy (Department for Education, 2019) to establish the 'golden thread'**
>
> 1. Create the right climate for leaders to establish supportive school cultures.
> 2. Transform support for early career teachers through an Early Career Framework.
> 3. Build a career offer that remains attractive to teachers as their careers and lives develop from the offer of new national professional qualifications.
> 4. Make it easier for great people to become teachers.
>
> Source: Ovenden-Hope & Kirkpatrick (2025)

The four commitments of the Teacher Recruitment and Retention Strategy identified above were intended to form the core of the 'golden thread' approach, and the success of these is explored in detail later in this chapter.

The 'golden thread of teacher development' (Department for Education, 2019) was 'hailed as one of the biggest policy success stories by those involved' (Dickens, 2024), with the ECF the 'jewel in the crown' (Dickens, 2024). Teachers, schools and politicians, while welcoming funded professional development for teachers, have challenged the controlled, prescribed and generic content of the ECF and questioned its efficacy for ECT development. In this chapter we explore and unpick the 'golden thread' to understand its contribution to the professional development of teachers in England since 2019.

Preparing for the 'golden thread of teacher development'?

Teacher development policy in England underwent significant changes between 2010 and 2018, focusing on ITT reforms, professional development initiatives, interventions to address recruitment and retention challenges, policy shifts and structural education changes. These policy changes aimed to improve teacher quality, increase school autonomy, and address recruitment and retention challenges in the teaching profession.

Teacher training and development changes in England, 2010–2018

1. Initial teacher training (ITT) reforms:
   - expansion of school-led ITT through the School Direct programme
   - encouragement of schools to become accredited providers of ITT (School Centred Initial Teacher Training – SCITTs)
   - allocation of ITT places only to providers rated 'good' or 'outstanding' by Ofsted
   - introduction of Troops to Teachers programme for former armed forces members.
2. Professional development initiatives:
   - introduction of new qualifications for school leaders – national professional qualifications for headship (NPQH), senior leadership (NPQSL) and middle leadership (NPQML)
   - establishment of a national network of teaching schools to develop leadership and raise teaching quality
   - creation of the Education Endowment Foundation to provide evidence-based teaching practices.
3. Recruitment and retention interventions:
   - introduction of training bursaries up to £25,000 for priority subjects
   - implementation of tax-free scholarships worth £25,000 in maths, chemistry, physics and computing
   - expansion of Teach First programme to increase high-achieving graduates in disadvantaged schools.

4. Policy shifts:

- reduction of bureaucracy to give teachers more professional autonomy
- reform of teacher appraisal and capability arrangements
- introduction of performance-related pay for classroom teachers.

5. Structural changes:

- expansion of the academies programme, giving schools more autonomy in teacher development
- scrapping of 20,000 pages of central guidance, to reduce bureaucracy.

Source: Department for Education (2015); Department for Education & Gibb (2017); Freedman (2022)

The policy changes for teacher professional development in England between 2010 and 2018 had mixed success, with some positive outcomes but also significant challenges. The increased focus on school-led training initiated by the government's 2010 White Paper, *The Importance of Teaching* (Department for Education, 2010), set out changes to shift teacher training towards a more school-led system (Universities UK, 2014). This led to the expansion of School Direct and School-Centred Initial Teacher Training (SCITT) programmes, which aimed to increase the proportion of time trainees spent in classrooms. The new schools-led policy approach for ITT created instability for many universities with established ITT provision through a drop in allocated trainee teacher numbers, a reduction in staff and a loss of experience in the teacher education discipline (Universities UK, 2014).

The introduction of new qualifications – the national professional qualifications (NPQs) for school leaders, including qualifications for headship (NPQH), senior leadership (NPQSL) and middle leadership (NPQML) – aimed to develop leadership and raise teaching quality (Department for Education, 2015). However, much of the CPD provided in England following the introduction of the NPQs did not meet all the criteria for high-quality professional development (Fletcher-Wood & Zuccollo, 2022). There were also reports of these changes to professional development having limited impact on student outcome, with an overall effect size of only 0.09 on student learning (Fletcher-Wood & Zuccollo, 2022).

The emphasis on evidence-based practices and the creation of the Education Endowment Foundation in 2011 aimed to support evidence-based teaching practices in schools, potentially improving the quality of professional development. There clearly has been a sector change in the use of evidence-based teaching in schools in England (Ovenden-Hope, 2024a), but concerns remain as to the relationship this has with the quality of teaching, as noted above. What is reported is that teachers in England were found to engage in less CPD than their international peers from 2010–2018. The 2018 TALIS data showed that England's secondary school teachers dedicated only 43 hours a year to professional development, below the OECD average of 62 hours (Fletcher-Wood & Zuccollo, 2022). It was also reported that 45% of secondary teachers felt they spent insufficient time on CPD (Fletcher-Wood & Zuccollo, 2022), indicating that the policy changes may not have adequately addressed teachers' professional development needs.

While the policy changes between 2010 and 2018 aimed to improve teacher professional development in England, their success was varied. The reforms succeeded in increasing school-led training and introducing new leadership qualifications. However, they failed to address the overall quantity and quality of CPD for teachers, with England lagging behind international averages. The impact on student outcomes was modest, and there were concerns about the stability of the initial teacher training sector. These mixed results suggest that further refinement of professional development policies was needed to fully achieve professional development that would engage teachers, enhance their practice, and encourage them to enter and stay in the profession.

Sewing the 'golden thread of teacher development'

Initial teacher training (ITT) is not long enough – if it happens at all since deregulation for academies, free schools and studio schools in 2012 and the appointment of unqualified teachers (HM Government, 2012) – to provide beginner teachers with the expertise they need to navigate the complexity of classroom teaching. It is impossible for trainee teachers that do undertake ITT to acquire all the necessary skills and knowledge to be a great teacher (Darling-Hammond, 2009), which makes teacher professional development essential. In 2019 the DfE acknowledged that beginning teachers lacked effective developmental opportunities at the start of their career (Department for Education, 2019), a time when learning generally takes a steep upward trajectory. It has been evidenced that beginning teachers are most likely to feel vulnerable, lack self-efficacy and think about leaving at the very start of their teaching career (Buchanan et al., 2013; Ginnis et al., 2018).

The DfE consulted with the newly established expert advisory group (Department for Education, 2018) for the Teacher Recruitment and Retention Strategy (Department for Education, 2019), which argued for the need to better equip beginning teachers with the skills to teach from the very start of their careers. Using the findings of the government consultation on strengthening qualified teacher status (QTS) and improving career progression for teachers that began in 2017, the expert advisory group advocated for structured support and development for newly qualified teachers (NQTs) (Department for Education, 2018). The findings of the 2018 report can be seen echoing in policy changes happening now for teacher development, as it outlined a clear continuum of progression from ITT through all career phases, with a need for credible in-service qualifications to compete with other professions, such as lawyers, doctors and accountants (Department for Education, 2018).

'Golden thread' strategy and reforms

Teacher Recruitment and Retention Strategy, 2019

Published by the DfE on 28 January 2019, prior to the Covid-19 pandemic, by the then education secretary, Damien Hinds, the Teacher Recruitment and Retention Strategy (Department for Education, 2019) was introduced to address the shortage of qualified secondary school teachers and to make the process of becoming a teacher easier. The document recognised that there were two main issues – teacher recruitment and teacher retention – and combined these within a single strategy (Universities' Council for the Education of Teachers, 2019). From a national perspective, the strategy aimed to answer two key questions:

1. How could teaching best be promoted as a profession to ensure recruitment targets were hit?
2. How could teachers in practice best be prevented from leaving the profession prematurely?

Support for the strategy was offered in the Foreword of the document by eight leading sector bodies, including teaching unions, Ofsted and the

Education Endowment Foundation (Department for Education, 2019). These bodies' representatives were typically familiar advisors used by the DfE to support new reforms and strategies in education (Ellis, 2024). The National Association of School-Based Teacher Trainers (NASBTT), a registered charity promoting schools-led training programmes, education and professional development of teachers, and the Universities' Council for the Education of Teachers (UCET), a national forum for the discussion of the education of teachers, were not part of the advisory panel. Therefore, the strategy was endorsed without the two professional bodies for ITT in England having any direct involvement in its development.

Five out of the ten advisory group members for the Teacher Recruitment and Retention Strategy were senior leaders of multi-academy trusts (MATs), and the other members were from the educational charities Teach First, the Institute for Teaching, and Ambition School Leadership (later, the latter two of these would merge to become one charity named Ambition Institute). MATs are trusts that receive state funding to run a number of schools free of local authority control. The make-up of the advisory board is important, as all the charities would go on to receive DfE funding for the delivery of the ECF and/or NPQs (Rowe, 2024).

The Teacher Retention and Recruitment Strategy (Department for Education, 2019) outlined four key commitments on which to focus, invest and reform. It was considered that these areas would have the biggest impact on improving teacher recruitment and retention, and would establish a 'golden thread' of professional development.

1. **Create the right climate for leaders to establish supportive school cultures:** This focus proposed a commitment to reform of the school accountability system and a reduction in teacher workload, with a simplification of the system to reduce data practices, remove floor standards and establish workload consideration in Ofsted judgements (Ofsted, 2019).
2. **Transform support for early career teachers:** The strategy had the development of the ECF (Department for Education, 2019a) as its core commitment. The ECF would give all beginning teachers, now to be called early career teachers (ECTs), a fully funded, two-year package of structured support, with time off timetabled teaching for two years and access to a mentor in school to support their professional development laid out by the ECF.
3. **Build a career offer that remains attractive to teachers as their careers and lives develop:** There was a proposal to support headteachers

in developing flexible working in schools, recognising the changing expectations of a work–life balance for professionals. There was also commitment to the development of specialist qualifications for non-leadership pathways through new national professional qualifications (NPQs). Along with the ECF, NPQs were to be a stitch in the 'golden thread of professional development'. NPQs were implemented in 2021 following a procurement process for lead providers. They were fully government funded for schools from September 2021 to September 2024, forming part of the £184 million Covid recovery plan that was running alongside education reform. At the time of writing, a review of the NPQs was planned for September 2025, to involve advisory groups, the DfE and the Education Endowment Foundation (EEF). Key objectives to be addressed in the review included:

- reduction of workload

- drawing on best practice for those teaching in special educational needs and disabilities (SEND) settings and the content for a new SENCO NPQ

- leadership progression across NPQs, and support with school operational aspects of leadership, such as finance and workforce.

4. **Make it easier for great people to become teachers:** There was an initial commitment to a new 'discover teaching initiative', but this did not happen. Instead, a new digital system to ease application to ITT was developed with a one-stop ITT application service. An ITT Market Review (Department for Education, 2021) was also launched to support ITT 'to work more efficiently and effectively' (Department for Education, 2019, p. 7). The ITT Market Review concluded in 2022, embedding standardisation, efficiency and evidence-based practice in pursuit of improved educational outcomes and teacher quality. This reform was noted by the government as a way of offering a seamless transition between initial teacher training and the next step for teachers, the ECF. It was an early indicator of policy intentions for an 'all through' teacher training and development experience that became legislation in 2024 with the ITTECF (Department for Education, 2024b).

The Teacher Recruitment and Retention Strategy set out a teacher career pathway of support, standards and qualifications for teachers and school leaders that were embedded within a 'golden thread' of professional development. Teachers' development and training would start with ITT and continue throughout their career into senior leadership (see Figure 3).

The stages of teachers' professional development were given an evidence base, overseen by the Education Endowment Foundation, to which all teachers would ascribe.

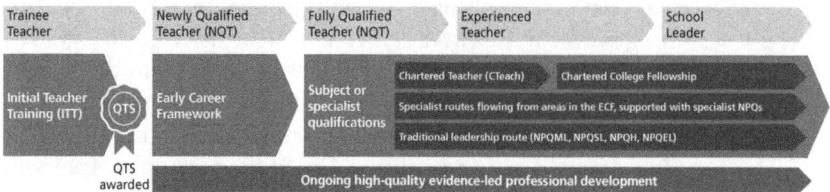

Figure 3: Teacher career pathway Source: Department for Education (2019, p. 27)

It could be argued that the reforms of the Teacher Recruitment and Retention Strategy (Department for Education, 2019) were the first to boldly display the neoliberal ideology of the government (Ovenden-Hope & Kirkpatrick, 2025). The 'performative' elements and 'managed' contracts of the ECF and NPQs, and the primacy of the 'market' and 'management' in the review of ITT (Ball, 2003), were clear indications of the way teacher education reform was manifesting.

During the delivery of the reforms set out in the Teacher Recruitment and Retention Strategy, additional reforms were added that affected teacher professional development and training. A brief overview of the reforms demonstrates that they embedded the standardisation and government control seen in the key teacher development reforms of the strategy. From ITT with a Core Content Framework, into the ECF and then on to the specialist NPQs, teachers' professional development was in the hands of the government and the shadow of a schools-led system.

The reforms that impacted on teacher professional development, but were not directly referenced in the Teacher Recruitment and Retention Strategy (Department for Education, 2019) include:

- a revised ITT Core Content Framework (CCF) (Department for Education, 2019c) that became mandatory in 2020 for all ITT training provider programmes, with ongoing revision and its eventual combining with the ECF for September 2025 (see chapter five for more on the ITTECF)
- the launch of teaching school hubs (87) in 2021 to provide 'centres of excellence for teacher training and development' (House of Commons, 2024, p. 9); the TSHs were used to deliver DfE-approved professional development only

- a National Institute of Teaching (NIoT) as the government's flagship organisation for the delivery of ITT, ECF, NPQs and the education research underpinning teacher professional development (Department for Education, 2021b)
- the policy paper, 'Delivering world-class teacher development', which heralded the 'golden thread of high-quality evidence underpinning the support, training and development available through the entirety of a teacher's career' (Department for Education, 2022c, p. 5); a DfE mantra emerged of 'teachers are made, not born' (Department for Education, 2022c, p. 5)
- the 'Opportunity for All' White Paper in 2022 (Secretary of State for Education, 2022b), which outlined a series of reforms stated to enhance the education system that included teacher development and recruitment; the ECF was presented as one of the key components of the government's strategy to provide 'an excellent teacher for every child', and ensure teachers have access to high-quality training and development throughout their careers (Secretary of State for Education, 2022).

The Early Career Framework, 2019

In 2018 the government realised that ECT attrition needed to be addressed, and began to explore ways to improve ECT retention through a new framework of support (Department for Education, 2018). Government consultations with an 'expert advisory group' (Department for Education, 2018) concluded that beginning teachers should be supported in their first years of teaching, to improve 'morale, satisfaction and retention' (Education Endowment Foundation, 2021a). There was an opportunity in the ECF teacher development reform being developed to align with the ITT core content guidance (Department for Education, 2019c), to create a standardised and fluid teacher development offer.

The ECF was identified in the Recruitment and Retention Strategy as priority 2 (Department for Education, 2019) and enacted as an explicit reform in 2019 (Department for Education, 2019a), for mandatory implementation in schools from September 2021. The ECF was never conceived as an assessment framework (Department for Education, 2019a). It was intended to support early career teachers (ECTs) through a mandatory school-based two-year focused training programme as part of their induction phase into teaching. The ECF was established to support ECTs becoming fully qualified against the Teachers' Standards (Department for Education, 2021d).

The ECF provided a national framework for a common induction with access to DfE-approved resources for all ECTs in state-funded schools. The government objective for the ECF was as a national standard in ECT professional development that would raise the status of teaching as a profession (House of Commons Education Committee, 2017). The ECF reform documents (Department for Education, 2019a; 2024c) compare teaching with medicine and law (Department for Education, 2019a, p. 4).

In September 2020 the DfE put out an invitation to tender for the national rollout of the ECF, with successful lead providers 'expected to develop and deliver a Full Induction Programme, based on the Core Induction Programmes' already available (Department for Education, 2022). Contracts were for four years, and each provider was expected to 'train' a minimum of 1,000 ECTs the following year, increasing to a minimum of 2,000 ECTs and their mentors from September 2022 (Department for Education, 2022). Training requirements for ECTs and mentors were prescribed by the DfE in the tender, to include a minimum of 18 hours of face-to-face training for ECTs and nine hours of face-to-face training for mentors, along with outlines of the core induction programmes, self-study and mentor sessions (Department for Education, 2022).

The procurement process for the lead providers of the ECF brought teacher development clearly into an education 'market,' with the 'business' of delivery being sought and won by a range of private companies, education charities and a university. The six accredited lead providers awarded contracts to deliver the full induction programmes of the ECF were Ambition Institute, Best Practice Network, Capita Business Services, Education Development Trust, Teach First and University College London Institute of Education (Department for Education, 2021a). In 2024 the lead providers' contracts came up for renewal, and were considered in the light of the DfE's review of the ECF (Department for Education, 2024d). Providers were asked to bid for a four-year renewal, and the outcomes were that the existing ECF providers Ambition Institute, Education Development Trust, Teach First and University College London Institute of Education were successful in being awarded renewed contracts. Best Practice Network, an existing ECF provider, was unsuccessful in its bid and the Teacher Development Trust, a national charity for effective teacher professional development, withdrew its bid to deliver the ECF and

NPQs. The NIoT continues to deliver the ECF but was exempt from the bidding process (Roberts & Nordern, 2024).

ECF policy on changes to statutory induction for ECTs was published in March 2021 for delivery in September 2021, demonstrating the rapid introduction for school implementation (Department for Education, 2021). This was all following a period of extreme adaptation and challenge for schools as they educated children through the Covid-19 pandemic. School leaders were expected to find resource in their systems to support significant changes to teacher development.

> The ECF changed professional development for ECTs in schools by giving them:
> - two years of evidence-based development from the start of their teaching career
> - 10% time off-timetable in year one of teaching, and 5% in the second year of teaching, to engage with their own professional development
> - access to a DfE-approved structured curriculum focusing on how teachers learn and what they learn
> - time with a school mentor to support them in becoming a teacher.

Mentors were given training to support them in their role with ECTs. Key figures in teacher education and school leaders that consulted with the government on teacher development requirements (Department for Education, 2018) heralded the ECF as a 'game changer' and the 'most significant reform to teaching in a generation' (Department for Education, 2019a, p. 20). Educationalists realised the importance of having government-funded professional development for beginning teachers, but with it came increasing government control of teacher development (Ellis, 2024). School leaders raised concerns that the content of the ECF was homogeneous, decontextualised and repetitive (Uttley, 2021) (which is how our teachers in chapter four identified their experience of the ECF). Professional bodies challenged the increase in workload for ECTs, mentors and school leaders (National Association of Head Teachers, 2021) (which was again corroborated by the teachers in our research shared in chapter four).

The ECF aimed to support ECTs and improve retention, however its (neoliberal) focus on standardisation, efficiency and market-oriented solutions was felt to limit its efficacy for ECT development (Department for Education, 2024d). In some ways, this initial period of the ECF was both 'the best of times and the worst of times' for ECT professional development. At the beginning there were comments on how the ECF had the 'potential to transform the support provided to recently qualified teachers in the first years of teaching' (Long & Danechi, 2021, p. 34) and was a 'triumph of consultative policy development' (Education Policy Institute, 2019, p. 100). Also, the ECF was intended to be delivered at no cost to the school, but there was a growing concern voiced by school leaders, ECTs, ECT mentors and teacher education professional bodies about how the ECF was being experienced in school (see chapter four for teachers' experiences of the ECF).

Key areas of discontent were emerging in the education sector; these included the workload for ECTs, the lack of flexibility in the framework to contextualise experience for ECTs, and the overlap between ITT programmes and the ECF (Department for Education, 2024d). In 2021, a survey of 6,661 teachers by the Chartered College of Teaching found that 75% of them felt ill-informed about the ECF (Chartered College of Teaching, 2021). The conclusion drawn was that schools were not given enough time by the government to prepare and inform their staff about this significant change in ECT development. The Chartered College of Teaching's findings suggest that schools were not ready for the rollout when it came. The pace of change also impacted on the lead providers, who were forced to develop the programmes and materials, as well as train their facilitators to train the ECTs and mentors, in six months (Ovenden-Hope, 2022).

Key outcomes of the government review of the ECF rollout

Workload

- Increased workload across school roles involved with the ECF due to unfamiliarity with the framework, especially in year one, and with multiple cohorts and dual roles for mentors and induction tutors.
- ECTs felt their workload was increased by ECF activities, and struggled with this and their wellbeing.
- Many mentors had additional roles in school, which added to their workload.

Complexity

- Managing the ECF for new cohorts of ECTs and changing mentors was challenging for lead providers, facilitators and induction tutors.
- Combining the role of mentor and induction tutor created tensions when supporting ECTs.

Confidence and understanding

- Mentors' confidence in understanding the delivery of the ECF increased, however there was less familiarity with the content (but increased confidence in delivery and content in year two for both mentor and ECT, as they were more familiar with framework).
- Both mentors and ECTs found the additional year (year two) of the framework beneficial, and in year two felt more confident and familiar with expectations from providers.
- Mentors were highly valued by ECTs throughout the ECF due to the support they provided.
- ECTs became more confident in assessment, planning and adaptive teaching as a consequence of engaging with the ECF.

Communication

- Both mentors and ECTs saw improvements from lead providers, delivery partners and appropriate bodies, with feedback given through surveys and lead provider monitoring visits.

Training and adaptions

- ECTs were generally positive about training, accessing provider platforms, and resources and progress monitoring.
- ECTs were positive about their ITT experiences and the ECF extended their learning, despite one-third of ECTs finding the ECF repetitive of ITT.

- Training lacked context-specific tailoring and subject-specific resources, which left mentors frustrated with the tailoring of the programme required and their increased workload.
- Mentors and ECTs felt there was a need for more flexibility in content and sequencing, with more of an awareness of ECT needs and school context.
- Overall, primary schools were more positive than secondary schools about ECF lead providers' programmes.

Source: Institute for Employment Studies & BMG Research (2024)

By 2023 concerns across the education sector about the ECF triggered a call for evidence by the DfE on both the Core Content Framework for ITT and the ECF (Department for Education, 2023a). The government published the response to the call for evidence in July 2023 (updated April 2024) (Department for Education, 2024e), which identified new evidence that would be included in a reformed Initial Teacher Training and Early Career Framework (ITTECF) (launched in January 2024) that offered a combined framework for ITT and the ECF for mandatory implementation in England in September 2025 (Department for Education, 2024b) and aimed to remedy the issues found. The ITTECF (Department for Education, 2024b) is discussed at length in chapter five. For more information on the ECF, please read *The Early Career Framework: Origins, Opportunities and Outcomes* (Ovenden-Hope, 2022).

Teacher experience case study

Mentor: second year as a mentor

I am in my fifth year of teaching and second year of mentoring. I have been offered lots of mentor CPD and coaching courses. It is nice to share experiences and expertise, and support beginner teachers in their teaching journeys. I have attended mentor training, and we have a good mentor community to reach out to. We have a drop-in once a term online and a face-to-face event at the end of the year. Historically, our school trust has run its own induction, but we have moved to the ECF and have colleagues completing NPQs with the same provider. This gives us a more streamlined approach to professional development and we feel that, by using the same provider, we have that continuity from ITT to leadership pathways. As a trust we are all on the same professional learning journey. We add any professional development to our trust system, Blue Sky, to monitor.

My knowledge of the Teacher Standards has improved from having an ECT. I am a non-teaching deputy, so have the flexibility within my timetable to support the ECF. My ECT has a subject mentor also. We did have some teething problems at the start of the ECF with getting everything set up and with different entry points. But I really like the ECF. It is clear and structured. I like the different sections, and it does provide support and supplement teaching. I like how content is sequenced and not released all at the same time.

I don't like mentioning the barriers of workload and time, but I feel they are always there, and it is for teachers to learn to manage. The guidance we received is that mentor meetings should happen outside of teaching hours and again this creates an issue of time. It is a hard balance. In school there are always a million things to do, but my role is to ensure the ECT ECF time is protected, working through the ECF with them and that they have the opportunity to observe good practice.

With staff following the 'golden thread' of ECF to NPQs with the same provider, we can provide this trust-wide, making sure they have protected time in the weekly timetable for meaningful meetings. I have worked with mentors in setting up agendas for the whole half term and to have identified a focus. We are a 'requires improvement' school, which makes it important to keep driving school improvement forwards, and this includes staff professional development.

If the mentor is effective, the ECTs receive a quality programme. I think we provide a good level of support and because many of us are completing our NPQ, and we've got the 'golden thread' running through our staff meetings, our understanding of professional development all links. We are seeing improvements in teaching due to the culture we are building in the school around professional development.

Conclusion: the last stitch of the golden thread

In 2023 the DfE commissioned Ofsted to conduct an independent review of teachers' professional development in schools (Department for Education, 2023). This review saw Ofsted examine the professional development received by teachers and school leaders since April 2021. Ofsted used the survey responses of 1,953 teachers and leaders and school visit meetings in 44 primary and secondary schools to draw conclusions on the efficacy of professional development in schools in England (Department for Education, 2023). His Majesty's Inspectors (HMI) concluded that the ECF and NPQs signified positive advancements in professional development. They reported that teachers are more research informed as a consequence of their ITT and therefore see value in professional development activities that are relevant to their practice and of high quality (Department for Education, 2023). Participation in the ECF and NPQs allowed for dedicated time for professional development, and ECTs wanted more opportunities to consult with other ECTs on the programme. Reporting specifically on those undertaking the ECF and NPQs, it was highlighted that there was a lack of flexibility with the programmes, mentor availability and poor, repetitive online provision as problems occurred. Face-to-face training opportunities were preferred over online training, and other teachers in school had little awareness of what the ECF and reformed NPQs actually were.

These findings from Ofsted (Department for Education, 2023) are not corroborated in wider research. Findings suggest that the Covid-19 pandemic made a significant impact on the professional development of teachers (Department for Education, 2023), as schools were able to offer increased online training. This was from a starting position of a weaker professional development offer in schools compared to other high-performing countries (House of Commons Education Committee, 2017). Teachers however felt the quality of online training was poor during Covid-19, and on return to school there was limited time for professional development due to staff absence and lesson cover (Department for Education, 2023). A report by UCL on ECT and mentor experiences of the ECF commented on the advantage of online learning for ECTs during Covid-19, and ECTs felt that they could attend online courses to increase subject knowledge as well as gain an enhanced understanding and knowledge of pastoral care (Qing et al., 2023). The English education system had been designed around accountability measures and data, making professional development a low priority (House of Commons Education Committee, 2017) until the ECF and NPQ reforms.

The connection between challenges in teacher recruitment and retention and diminishing entitlement to high-quality, sustained professional development changed the government's approach to teacher CPD. The 'golden thread' was intended to provide a suite of professional development that would not only improve the quality of teaching in schools but also assist retention because the teacher's entitlement to career-progressing development was clear and accessible (Sims et al., 2021). However, the 'golden thread' will only work if the professional development underpinning it is effective in design, delivery and content. In the box below we outline the characteristics of effective professional development as a minimum entitlement for all teachers. For ECTs there should always be the additional support of a mentor who has time to support and guide them through their first years as a teacher.

Characteristics of effective professional development

- Peer support
- Opportunities for collaboration/coaching with professional colleagues
- Dedicated time
- Taught workshops
- Evidence-informed practice
- Understanding and commitment to professional learning
- Professional reflective practice
- Development of Professional Learning Communities (PLCs)

Source: Cordingley (2015); Ovenden-Hope et al. (2018)

Ideally, the ECF could be an active process of inquiry for ECTs, with experienced teachers participating in this inquiry as mentors and induction tutors, a community of practice working together to improve professional learning running alongside the golden thread of development. Initial teacher training should provide a high-quality, rigorous initial preparation for teaching, with a structured curriculum and evidence-informed training approaches that introduce the 'golden thread of professional development' that is yet to come. Teaching can be a long and rewarding career, and progression in that career should be supported by qualifications that give agency through skills and knowledge acquisition that can be applied to practice (and one day the wider education system). The reformed NPQs provided more subject-specific and pedagogical development, and after three years of funding many teachers felt the loss of this entitlement.

The last stitch of the 'golden thread' *is* teacher entitlement to high-quality professional development throughout their career. A publication by the Church of England outlines its hopes for teachers to flourish in their careers, with the desire to want to stay in teaching, feeling satisfied and confident in the work that they do to support pupil learning (Church of England, 2023). Our hope is that the ITTECF (Department for Education, 2024b) and the recognition by the Labour government of Early Career Teacher Entitlement (ECTE) will create the supportive culture in schools that was a commitment of the Teacher Recruitment and Retention Strategy back in 2019. The government has pledged to review the ECF in 2027, which brings optimism for ECTE, as there is potential to create a meaningful, contextualised career-long professional development that supports teacher agency and autonomy. We hope career-long teacher entitlement is also considered.

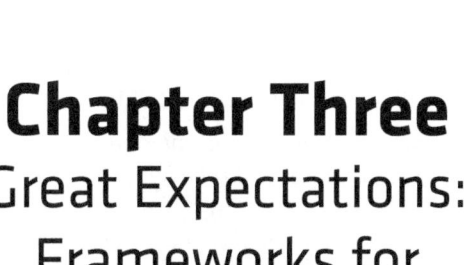

Chapter Three
Great Expectations: Frameworks for 'great teaching'

I have been bent and broken, but – I hope – into a better shape.

Charles Dickens, *Great Expectations* (1861, p. 646)

Introduction

There is hope to be found in the works of Charles Dickens, and this hope springs from the personal growth and resilience of some of his characters. Adversity and challenges are tools for transformation. This route to self-knowledge and purpose is extreme, yet many teachers have reported feelings that align with being 'bent and broken' by the ECF (see chapter four). We have 'great expectations' of any enhanced Early Career Teacher Entitlement (ECTE) that may come from the 2027 review of the ECF, and a hope that, until then, the ITTECF will leave our teachers in 'better shape'.

In England, the notion of a 'great teacher' and/or 'great teaching' has been embedded in education policy and reform for teacher development. The 'golden thread of teacher development' (see chapter two) is spun with yarn intended to support and develop 'great teachers'. The Education Endowment Foundation (EEF), a charitable organisation funded by the government to develop education interventions that close the gap in attainment for children from socioeconomically disadvantaged backgrounds, published its *Effective Professional Development* guidance report in 2021. In the Foreword, the chief executive of the EEF, Professor Rebecca Francis, reiterated the link between quality teaching, teacher quality and effective professional development:

Supporting high quality teaching is pivotal in improving children's outcomes. Indeed, research tells us that high quality teaching can narrow the disadvantage gap. It is therefore hugely encouraging to see a host of new initiatives and reforms that recognise the importance of teacher quality such as the Early Career Framework and the new national professional qualifications. These exemplify a growing consensus that promoting effective professional development plays a crucial role in improving classroom practice and pupil outcomes.

Education Endowment Foundation (2021, p. 4)

In 2022, the Conservative government was confident that the reformed teacher development frameworks providing the minimum entitlement to beginning and established teachers mentioned by Allen (Education Endowment Foundation, 2021) – the CCF (Department for Education, 2019c), the ECF (Department for Education, 2019a) and NPQs (Department for Education, 2020) – would deliver 'great teachers' and quality teaching for schools.

Teachers are the foundation of the education system – there are no great schools without great teachers. The quality of teaching is the single most important in-school factor for improving pupil outcomes.

Department for Education (2022, p. 4)

What is 'great teaching'?

But what is a 'great teacher' and what makes 'great teaching'? The government's great expectations of the teacher development frameworks for school improvement are based on a relatively nebulous concept. There is no single, comprehensive definition of 'great teachers' or 'great teaching'. Government education policies suggest that a 'great teacher' is characterised by expertise, continuous improvement, high expectations of students, and impact on student outcomes (see the accompanying box, *Government policy characteristics of a 'great teacher'*).

> **Government policy characteristics of a 'great teacher'**
>
> 1. Expertise: possessing strong subject knowledge and pedagogical skills.
> 2. High expectations: setting ambitious goals for all students and working to help them achieve these standards.
> 3. Continuous improvement: engaging in ongoing professional development and training.
> 4. Impact: significantly improving student outcomes, with research suggesting that highly effective teachers can raise each pupil's attainment by a third of an examination grade.
>
> Source: Department for Education (2022a; 2022b); House of Commons Education Committee (2012); Secretary of State for Education (2022)

Government documents, policies and reforms have emphasised the importance of 'great teachers' since 2012 (House of Commons Education Committee, 2012), but a 2014 report examining the evidence informing 'great teaching' ensured that teacher development frameworks, moving forward, would sustain the concept of developing 'great teachers'.

'What makes great teaching?'

In 2014 Rob Coe and colleagues, working for the Centre of Evaluation and Monitoring, Durham University and the Sutton Trust, launched a report titled 'What makes great teaching?' (Coe et al., 2014). The report established 'great teaching' as an indicator for quality teaching and effective teaching in schools, and supporting 'great teachers' as the goal for professional development frameworks.

Great teaching is defined as that which leads to improved student progress.

Coe et al. (2014, p. 2)

The report recognised that 'defining effective teaching is not easy' but that the research demonstrated that 'student progress is the yardstick by which teacher quality should be assessed' (Coe et al., 2014, p. 2). The report went on to identify 'six components of great teaching' that should be used as a 'starter kit' for assessing teaching quality: (Pedagogical) Content Knowledge, Quality of Instruction, Classroom Climate, Classroom Management, Teacher Beliefs, and Professional Behaviours (see box). All six of these components of 'great teaching' are used by the 'very best teachers' when demonstrating 'effective pedagogy' (Coe et al., 2014, p. 2).

The six components of 'What makes great teaching?'

The 'What makes great teaching?' report (Coe et al., 2014) offers a research-informed perspective on defining and promoting 'great teaching'. Its central argument is that effective teaching is defined by improved student progress and outcomes that matter for their future success. The concept of great teaching is used for assessing teacher quality.

The report identifies six components of great teaching, ranked by the strength of evidence supporting their impact on student outcomes:

1. (Pedagogical) Content Knowledge: deep understanding of the subject matter and how students learn it.
2. Quality of Instruction: effective questioning, assessment, modelling, practice and scaffolding.
3. Classroom Climate: positive interactions, high expectations, and valuing effort and resilience.
4. Classroom Management: efficient use of time and resources, and consistent behaviour management.
5. Teacher Beliefs: understanding of learning theories and the role of teaching.
6. Professional Behaviours: reflection, professional development, collaboration and communication with parents.

All six components will be demonstrated by the 'very best teachers'.

Source: Coe et al. (2014)

Chapter Three: Great Expectations

The report also explored 'frameworks for capturing teaching quality' (Coe et al., 2014, p. 25), emphasising the need for multiple measures and triangulation of evidence across these frameworks. Six key approaches to the measuring of teaching quality, or great teachers, were identified:

1. Classroom observations: by peers, principals, or external evaluators
2. Value-added models: assessing gains in student achievement
3. Student ratings
4. Principal (headteacher) judgement
5. Teacher self-reports
6. Analysis of classroom artefacts and teacher portfolios.

Classroom observations, value-added models and student ratings were identified in the report as demonstrating moderate validity in signalling teacher effectiveness. Classroom observations are clearly embedded into teacher development frameworks in England, and the value-added models have been a core part of teacher accountability for effectiveness.

The importance of formative assessment and feedback for teacher development was highlighted in the report (Coe et al., 2014), with the evaluation of teaching framed as a continuous professional learning opportunity. The need for high-quality observation protocols, trained observers and pooling results from multiple observations was emphasised as a tool to understand teacher effectiveness. This framework of teacher development recognised the importance of a teacher 'knowledge-building cycle', where feedback on teaching and subsequent changes in practice led to improved student outcomes (Coe et al., 2014, p. 40). The notion that teachers plateau after their first few years of teaching was challenged, with supportive professional environments being championed as the way to foster continued professional development for 'great teaching'.

The six principles of teacher feedback

The six principles of teacher feedback provided in 'What makes great teaching?' (2014) offered clear guidance for school leaders and mentors that can still be seen in professional development frameworks today:

1. Focus on improving student outcomes.
2. Relate feedback to clear, specific and challenging goals.
3. Focus on learning rather than personal comparisons.

4. Encourage independent learning.

5. Mediate feedback with a mentor in a supportive environment.

6. Promote a culture of professional learning and support.

Source: Coe et al. (2014)

The outcome-oriented approach to 'great teaching' of the 'What makes great teaching?' report (Coe et al., 2014) provided a standard for supporting and measuring teacher quality that has significantly influenced the development of England's teacher education and professional development frameworks, and the language used within them. The CCF, ECF and NPQs, and the ITTECF, have all incorporated key principles and evidence-based practices identified in the report.

Influence on the Core Content Framework

Evidence-based teaching practices highlighted as effective in the Coe et al. (2014) report have clearly influenced content in the Core Content Framework (CCF) for Initial Teacher Training (ITT). Key elements of the report identifiable in the CCF include:

- incorporation of 'Learn that …' statements, which are directly aligned with the ECF, ensuring consistency in the evidence base for both trainee and early career teachers
- focus on behaviour management, identified as crucial by the Carter Review (Carter, 2015) and supported by the 'What makes great teaching?' report's emphasis on classroom management
- emphasis on subject and pedagogical knowledge, reflecting the report's identification of these as top components of great teaching.

The impact on the Early Career Framework of 'What makes great teaching?'

The ECF has been significantly influenced by the Coe et al. (2014) report, as evidenced by the:

- structured two-year support package for early career teachers, focusing on evidence-based practices
- alignment of 'Learn that …' statements with the best available research evidence, mirroring the approach in the CCF

- emphasis on mentoring and dedicated time for professional development, reflecting the report's recommendations on effective teacher feedback and continuous learning.
- significant investment (at least £130 million annually) to support ECF delivery, indicating the government's commitment to evidence-based teacher development.

Influence on national professional qualifications

The national professional qualifications (NPQs) have been reformed to incorporate insights from the Coe et al. (2014) report and align with the broader teacher development reforms:

- creation of a 'golden thread' of teacher development, ensuring consistency from ITT through to leadership roles (see chapter two)
- reform of existing qualifications (senior leadership, headship, and executive leadership) to reflect the latest evidence on effective leadership and teaching practices
- introduction of new specialist NPQs to replace the previous middle leadership qualification, focusing on specific areas of expertise
- emphasis on evidence-based practice and the application of research findings in leadership roles.

These frameworks collectively demonstrate an embedding of the report's recommendations, with the intention of creating a coherent system of teacher development based on robust evidence of what constitutes 'great teaching'. The ongoing evaluation of these frameworks, particularly the ECF and NPQs, suggests a commitment to continuous improvement, and responsiveness to emerging research and practitioner feedback.

Implications for the Early Career Framework from 'What makes great teaching?'

There were recommendations for the support of 'great teaching' in the 'What makes great teaching?' report (Coe et al., 2014) that are either notably absent from recent teacher development reforms or have been diluted in their use. These omissions should be considered for future entitlement. The ECF aims to provide a structured programme of support and development for ECTs and will continue to do so within the ITTECF. Drawing on the Coe et al. (2014) report, several areas for potential enhancement to the ECF can be identified to improve ECT entitlement in the future:

- **Strengthening the focus on pedagogical content knowledge:** The ECF should ensure that ECTs develop a deep understanding of the subjects they teach, including common misconceptions and effective strategies for addressing them. Mentors should be equipped to support ECTs in developing this crucial aspect of their practice.
- **Enhancing the quality of instructional coaching:** The ECF should prioritise evidence-based instructional strategies, such as effective questioning, assessment for learning, modelling and scaffolding. Mentors should receive training in these strategies and how to support ECTs in implementing them effectively.
- **Promoting a positive classroom climate:** The ECF should emphasise the importance of building positive relationships with students, setting high expectations and fostering aspirations. Mentors can help ECTs develop strategies for creating a supportive and inclusive classroom environment.
- **Developing effective classroom management skills:** The ECF should provide ECTs with practical strategies for managing student behaviour, maximising learning time and creating a well-organised classroom. Mentors can offer guidance and support in implementing these strategies.
- **Fostering reflective practice and professional growth:** The ECF should encourage ECTs to reflect on their teaching practice, seek feedback from mentors and colleagues, and engage in CPD. The six principles of teacher feedback outlined above would serve as a valuable guide for mentors.
- **Ensuring high-quality mentoring:** The ECF's success hinges on the quality of mentoring provided to ECTs. Mentors should be experienced teachers with a strong track record of effectiveness. They should receive adequate training and support to fulfil their role effectively.
- **Focus on student outcomes:** The ECF should encourage ECTs to focus on improving student outcomes and use data to inform their teaching practice. Mentors can help ECTs analyse student data and identify areas for improvement.

The notion of 'quality' in teaching

The Coe et al. (2014) report aligned 'great teaching' with teaching quality, as well as teaching effectiveness. However, the notion of quality in teaching should be unpacked further to understand how it affects teacher development frameworks and teacher development opportunities within them.

'Quality' in teaching is a notion used by the DfE to explain performance, justify focused types of professional development (such as the CCF, ECF and NPQs) and generally explain why some schools serve their students better than others (Coe et al., 2014; Sutton Trust, 2011). There is a general consensus that high-quality teaching has a positive impact on learning, particularly for students from disadvantaged backgrounds, who are said to gain approximately one and a half years' worth of learning in one school year when taught by a good teacher, as opposed to only half a year's worth of learning with a poor teacher (Allen & Sims, 2018). However, as identified above, there appears to be no agreed or commonly used definition of 'great' or 'good' or 'quality' teaching (Kime, 2015; Steadman & Ellis, 2021).

The lack of definition for quality teaching is challenging and appears as nebulous as the concept of 'great teaching' discussed above. Referring to 'quality teaching' becomes even more problematic due to the difficulty in distinguishing between *teacher* quality and *teaching* quality (Ovenden-Hope et al., 2022). The proxy for quality is often 'effectiveness' (Skourdoumbis, 2017), as we have seen in the influential 'What makes quality teaching?' report (Coe et al., 2014). Using effectiveness as an indicator of quality teaching has been contentious when understanding professional development.

There are also clearly limitations in judging effectiveness [of teaching] through the narrow window of pupil outcomes.

Madgwick (2020, para. 18, lines 1–2)

Equating effectiveness with quality when examining teachers and/or teaching has been argued to be an economistic view that 'prioritises the relationship between teachers and student achievement' (Steadman & Ellis, 2021, p. 2). The difficulty with this is that student achievement is most typically assessed by the outcomes of high-stakes assessments (Greaves et al., 2019), which can be impacted by many variables, including many teachers' contribution to learning over time. Isolating the way a single teacher's quality, or the quality of their teaching over time, on a student's GCSE examination outcome is practically impossible. Trusted educational charities that focus on evidence-based research adopt this circumscribed view of quality. The EEF online Teaching and Learning Toolkit evaluates strategies to improve teaching and learning by assessing the average impact they have on pupil attainment, and the Sutton Trust directly attributes pupil attainment to the improvement of teacher effectiveness (Sutton Trust, 2011).

Measuring quality teaching

Accepting that 'quality', like 'great', is a challenging concept to articulate clearly when considering teaching and teachers, attempting to measure the quality of teaching is equally fraught with inconsistencies. Different methods for measuring teaching quality include, but are not limited to, classroom observation, student perception surveys, stakeholder views, and interrogating data or artefacts, all of which have mixed outcomes (Grigg, 2015). Considering the six elements of teacher feedback to support 'great teaching' identified above (Coe et al., 2014), these opportunities for supporting professional development in teachers have become a tool for measuring their 'effectiveness' or quality in the classroom. The move between teacher feedback and measurement is complex, as variations in 'ratings' caused by different interpretations of the same behaviours, or by different conceptualisations of aspects of instruction (Lindorff et al., 2020), offer imperfect data on teaching quality.

As suggested above when discussing the relationship between teaching/teachers and student outcomes, measuring the quality of teaching through pupil achievement or progress data is problematic (Kime, 2015; Muijs & Reynolds, 2018). It is incredibly difficult to identify and control factors that impact pupil progress and achievement (Grigg, 2015). Added to this is that the way the roles of teacher and learner are understood can influence perceptions of what is, or what is not, quality teaching, and this may influence what to measure and how to measure it (Grigg, 2015). Policymakers and educational organisations working directly with the government have continued to emphasise the use of pupil achievement as a measure of teaching quality.

Measuring the quality of teaching and of teachers by student achievement carries huge risks. Being located within a neoliberal economistic ideology, it assumes a causality that is impossible to measure but is assumed to exist. If teacher development entitlement is 'held to account' by this measure,

Chapter Three: Great Expectations

it will not succeed, and any government investment will be removed. Therefore, the government needs to reconsider how to measure the quality of teaching to evaluate the effectiveness of teacher development. Our fear is that the government in England will expect student achievement to increase concurrently with its investment in 'the golden thread of teacher development' reforms implemented from 2021, and if this is not evidenced, then the ECF and NPQs will be assumed to have been ineffective.

While there may be a lack of consensus about what quality teaching is and how to measure it, no one would argue that improvements in teaching quality aligned to the principles of 'great teaching' noted above are not worth pursuing within a teacher's professional development entitlement.

Teacher experience case study

Early Career Teacher: career changer

I was in fashion design for 15 years until the pandemic hit, when there was a realisation that this industry was more tailored for a younger person with the travel. You rarely see old designers. So I thought it was probably the right time to take a big pay cut and go into teaching.

I'm very passionate about the area I teach. My strengths as an ECT are that I can apply my experiences in design to the classroom, and from early observations my classroom is calm and purposeful. I have high expectations and good classroom management, which adds to a positive environment, and I think encourages pupils to take risks. One of my weaknesses is not breaking information down into more manageable chunks instead of information overload.

Our ECF provider is Best Practice Network (BPN). I have a mentor in my subject area, and we meet once a week to discuss the training and what's happened in school. There's also a professional mentor that looks after all ECTs. I did my PGCE at the school I now work at. At the end of year one of the ECF I would say I'm possibly a little more confident in my subject knowledge, as I had to rewrite the scheme of work over the summer for key stage 3.

I have become more confident the more I teach the topics, and can change things if they don't work. I have been through the moderation process for examination years. It's taken time to learn as we have worked through the different modules of the ECF in more depth. I still think they could align the whole teaching standards versus ECF modules and understand more of the theory through doing.

I haven't had any experience of other induction programmes, but I have a good mentor, and having the structure in place of protected time and knowing it is the case for two years helps. It is a shame we have only had one face-to-face meeting with other ECTs as at times you feel on your own, so networking would have helped.

In terms of negatives of the framework, there needs to be more flexibility. It's like 'right, the focus is on this' and my identified focus is completely different. My mentor and I have adapted to find a way that suits us away from the rigid structure and more realistic to teaching and everyday practice. An example of this occurred when I needed to run a trip, and we used the mentor meeting time to go through the paperwork.

Auditing of the ECT's skills needs to happen at the start of the ECF and then it can improve on the flexibility of the content. I wouldn't say my subject knowledge is secure yet after two years. I feel the time could have been used to focus on areas of my teaching that my mentor and I could identify instead of going through six pages of reading. The ECF is definitely overwhelming for an ECT. I get the intention, in terms of feeling supported and that beginner teachers need structure, but that's what the mentor is for.

My mentor comes and observes me for 15–20 minutes each week, and we follow the BPN weekly guide on auditing knowledge and pick five things I want to work on. We have a conversation about this and reflect on weekly targets. The update is more of a general overview of the week. Some of the content we just tick without completing.

I am a workaholic, so commenting on workload is a terrible question for me to answer. My mentor says I will burn out, but I've literally been working this hard for 15 years now. Part of the increased workload is necessary with the new scheme of work and trying to embed some of the ECF. My mentor is aware I am teaching more than I should, and we prioritise mentor meetings. I want to discuss real-life scenarios and areas of learning that will benefit my actual practice (such as coursework moderating and revision techniques) in the mentor meetings. I think this is what will make me a great teacher.

Other ECTs comment a lot about workload and working conditions, and can't believe I left a high-paid job to come into teaching. I enjoy teaching and don't see myself leaving.

In year two of the ECF I found there were fewer meetings and I had a new mentor as my old one went on maternity leave. I missed the subject-specific help with the new mentor, so I enrolled on a textiles course. Year two was definitely more repetitive, basic content and covered a lot of content from the PGCE. The 'genericness' has been less helpful and if you need further support you speak to other colleagues in your school. Year two definitely felt like a tick-box exercise and move on.

I have worked on maintaining high expectations and my subject knowledge has improved from teaching different year groups. I've tweaked how I teach things. I've written all the schemes of work I'm teaching, and I have found my way. The strengths in my teaching have come from classroom experience rather than the ECF. There's no specific subject knowledge in the framework. We had to do an action research project as part of the ECF and I was doing this already in school, so tied it in with DT and working on rotations. I am the only fashion and textiles teacher.

The induction tutor does an observation once a term. She sends through reminders about things that we need to do, like school visits, and how to go about these. She will give us updates on the ECF also. I think experiences of the ECF vary depending on your school, or what support network you have, or if you are struggling more. In year two it feels like another thing to do.

I get non-contact time for the ECF, but in reality my 5% is, like, two hours a fortnight or something. One of those hours is my mentor meeting so that gives me one hour, and then two hours after school every so often you have face-to-face training, plus logging into Canvas. So I get the two hours, but spend more time than that on the ECF requirements. In terms of workload, if you want people to fully engage and invest, you need to give them the time to do it. And the reality in my situation is two hours a fortnight isn't enough. I don't know where people are finding the time to engage with it and people in teaching are going to burn out. I am a career changer and used to regularly working 60-hour weeks, and being an ECT is hard for me!

The face-to-face training is PowerPoint based, and the slides are talked through. You can literally see the transcript being used by the facilitator, of the training that they have been told by the provider to talk through. There tends to be a lot of discussion on our table, and she mixes us up with different people, but it is very much the same delivery model of 'work through the PowerPoint', 'ask some questions' and 'have a discussion'. The ECF needs to be tailored more to what people require. In our training, for example, there are a lot of ECTs. I sit with a PE teacher and a maths teacher in a primary school, and I am a textiles teacher in a secondary school. We all have very different needs as to how we want to approach teaching. The genericness of it really hinders its purpose and you don't get anything out of it. So then it feels like an extra workload. We sit there and ponder, and then someone asks, 'Do you have a reflection journal?' I'm like, 'I haven't eaten all day.' I walk out of my lesson and think, 'That wasn't great, and I need to do something about it.' Allow ECTs the time. And the whole online portal, it's reading and tick boxes. I don't know what people are getting out of that.

From coming from the world of fashion, in education there seems a lot of unnecessary admin, and the inefficiency of systems is archaic in my opinion, and the yearly reviews. I've worked in the best companies in the world, which are forward-thinking, and the concept of filling out a four-page form that shows evidence that you've done your job is bonkers!

A Core Content Framework (CCF) for 'great teachers'?

The Core Content Framework (CCF), introduced in 2019 and implemented from September 2021, represents a significant shift in the approach to initial teacher training in England (Department for Education, 2019c). This framework defines the minimum entitlement for all trainee teachers and is designed to provide a foundation upon which new teachers can build their careers.

The CCF is structured around eight key areas: setting high expectations, promoting good progress, demonstrating good subject and curriculum knowledge, planning and teaching well-structured lessons, adapting teaching, making accurate and productive use of assessment, managing behaviour effectively, and fulfilling wider professional responsibilities (Department for Education, 2019c). This approach aims to ensure that all newly qualified teachers enter the profession with a consistent baseline of knowledge and skills.

It has been argued that one of the strengths of the CCF is its alignment with current research evidence. The framework was developed in consultation with the Education Endowment Foundation (EEF) and other sector representatives, to support the embedding of contemporary understanding of effective teaching practices. It has been argued that while an evidence-based approach is crucial in developing 'great teachers', the limitation of the evidence base used, and the prescriptive content of the CCF 'curriculum' merely serves to sustain an outcomes-driven model of teacher development, with little flexibility for trainee teachers to engage with, and choose from, a range of teaching and learning approaches and skills to apply in a context-rich environment (Brooks, 2021).

This critique of the CCF raises important questions about the balance between providing a consistent foundation for all trainee teachers and allowing for the flexibility needed to address diverse educational contexts. Furthermore, the CCF's focus on a 'minimum entitlement' may inadvertently lead to a narrowing of ITT content. While the framework is intended as a baseline, there is a risk that ITT providers, particularly those new to the role following the ITT Market Review (Department for Education, 2021), may focus primarily on meeting these minimum requirements rather than offering a broader, more comprehensive training experience. This could potentially limit the development of 'great teachers' who require a more nuanced and expansive understanding of education.

The influence of education policy on the CCF is evident in its emphasis on evidence-based practice, the use of a government-funded organisation to curate the evidence informing the curriculum, and its alignment with the Teachers' Standards. This reflects the broader policy shift since 2010 towards standardisation and accountability in teacher education (Ovenden-Hope & Kirkpatrick, 2024). This standardisation of trainee teacher experience through the CCF may come at the cost of innovation and diversity in teacher training approaches and a reduction in the number of opportunities to develop 'great teachers'.

An Early Career Framework (ECF) for 'great teachers'?

The Early Career Framework (Department for Education, 2019a), introduced alongside the CCF in 2021, represented a significant extension of development entitlement for ECTs in England. The ECF provided a structured two-year induction period, replacing the previous one-year newly qualified teacher (NQT) programme. This reform reflected the recognition that the transition from trainee to fully qualified teacher requires sustained support and development, essential in the development of 'great teachers'.

A key strength of the ECF is its comprehensive approach to early career development. The framework covers a range of key areas, including behaviour management, pedagogy, curriculum, assessment and professional responsibilities (Department for Education, 2019a). This broad teacher development coverage aimed to ensure that ECTs continue to develop their skills and knowledge across all aspects of their role.

The ECF also demonstrated a commitment to evidence-based practice, with its content aligned with current research approved by the EEF for effective teaching (Education Endowment Foundation, 2021). This approach helps to support ECT exposure to strategies and techniques that have been shown to improve student outcomes, but sustains the outcomes-driven perception of 'quality teaching'. The framework's emphasis on mentoring and structured support also aligns with research highlighting the importance of these factors in teacher retention and development.

The ECF has faced some challenges following implementation. The increased workload for both ECTs and their mentors has been a concern, with some arguing that the additional requirements may actually hinder rather than support teacher development (see chapter four). The structured nature of the ECF has been argued to have led to a 'tick-box' approach to professional development (Ovenden-Hope & Kirkpatrick, 2024), rather than fostering genuine reflection and growth, qualities of a 'great teacher' and effective teacher development (Cordingley et al., 2015).

The influence of education policy on the ECF is clear, acting as part of a broader strategy to address teacher shortages and improve the overall quality of teaching in England (Department for Education, 2019c). The ECF reflects a policy shift towards viewing teacher development as a continuum in developing 'great teachers' as part of a 'golden thread of development', rather than a process that ends with initial qualification.

National professional qualifications (NPQs) for 'great teachers'?

National professional qualifications (NPQs) represented the next stage in the teacher development continuum, focusing on leadership and specialisation. The revised suite of NPQs, introduced alongside the CCF and ECF, aimed to provide a coherent pathway of minimum entitlement for teacher career progression to support 'great teachers' throughout their career (Department for Education, 2020).

The NPQs cover a range of specialisations, including leading teacher development, which directly supported the implementation of the ECF. This alignment between different stages of teacher development is a strength of the framework, promoting consistency and continuity in professional learning, essential in the support of 'great teachers'. It also reflected a policy shift by offering qualifications in different areas, including leading behaviour and culture; the NPQs acknowledged that 'great teachers' can have impact beyond their own classrooms.

A key feature of the NPQs was the focus on the practical application of knowledge and skills. The qualifications were designed to be directly relevant to teachers' and school leaders' roles, with a strong emphasis on implementing learning in the school context. This approach helped to ensure that the development of 'great teachers' was not just theoretical but had a tangible impact on school improvement (in line with the outcomes-driven foundation of the teacher development reforms).

The NPQs have faced criticism for potentially creating a narrow view of leadership development. The prescribed nature of the qualifications, as with the CCF and ECF, was found not to adequately address the diverse contexts in which school leaders operate (Department for Education, 2024).

There is also a risk that the focus on specific qualifications could lead to a 'credentialism' in education leadership, where formal qualifications are prioritised over practical experience and contextual understanding (which may be better served by another training or development opportunity outside of the government approved and funded suite of NPQs).

The influence of education policy on the NPQs is evident in their alignment with broader school improvement strategies. The qualifications are designed to support the development of leaders who can implement evidence-based practices and drive school-wide improvement. This reflects a policy emphasis on distributed leadership and the role of middle leaders in school effectiveness, and the sustained approach to outcomes-driven teacher development.

The Initial Teacher Training and Early Career Framework (ITTECF) for 'great teachers'?

The Initial Teacher Training and Early Career Framework (ITTECF), which became mandatory in England from September 2025, represents an evolution in the approach to teacher development and support for beginning teachers in England. The new framework combines and replaces the previously separate Initial Teacher Training Core Content Framework (CCF) and Early Career Framework (ECF), aiming to provide a more coherent and comprehensive development pathway and minimum entitlement to professional development for teachers at the start of their career (Department for Education, 2024b).

The ITTECF is designed to cover teacher training and induction periods spanning at least three years. It sets out the entitlement of every trainee and ECT to a core body of knowledge, skills and behaviours that define 'great teaching'. Key features of the framework maintain the established approaches (and associated challenges) of the CCF and ITT, with content based on EEF-approved 'best available evidence' only, and a broad 'curriculum' that encompasses all aspects of teaching considered appropriate to the stage of a trainee's or ECT's development. These features are intended to ensure preparedness for the next stage in the beginning teacher's professional development, but as we have seen with the forerunner frameworks, the controlled content can restrict and reduce teacher development.

The ITTECF does offer the potential for greater flexibility than the CCF and ECF. While providing a minimum entitlement, the ITTECF allows accredited ITT providers and ECF lead providers to integrate additional analysis and critique of theory, research and expert practice as they identify is appropriate to the beginning teacher's needs. Content for trainee teachers and ECTs is subject and phase agnostic, with providers expected to tailor the application to specific contexts (Department for Education, 2024b).

Alignment of the ITTECF with the concept of 'great teachers'

The ITTECF's approach to developing 'great teachers' is evident in several aspects of the reform:

- **Continuous development:** By combining ITT and ECF, the framework emphasises that becoming a 'great teacher' is a continuous process that extends beyond initial training.

- **Evidence-informed practice:** The focus on evidence-based teaching strategies aligns with the notion that 'great teachers' should be well versed in effective pedagogical approaches.

- **Adaptability:** The framework promises flexibility that allows for the development of teachers who can adapt their practice to different contexts and student needs.

- **Comprehensive skill set:** The ITTECF covers a wide range of teaching aspects, reflecting the multifaceted nature of great teaching.

The ITTECF demonstrates continuity with previous education policies on teacher development entitlement, while also introducing some key enhancements based on review outcomes of the CCF and ECF (Department for Education, 2023a; 2024d):

- **Extended support:** The framework maintains and reinforces the commitment to providing structured support for teachers beyond their initial training, a principle established in the previous ECF.

- **Streamlined approach:** By combining the CCF and ECF, the ITTECF addresses feedback about unnecessary repetition between initial training and early career development.

- **Focus on evidence:** The continued emphasis on evidence-based practice aligns with the trend in recent education policies to ground teacher development in research.
- **Addressing content gaps:** The new framework includes updated content on supporting pupils with special educational needs and disabilities (SEND), high-quality oral language, early cognitive development and children's mental health, reflecting evolving priorities in education practice.
- **Reduced workload for mentors:** In response to concerns about mentor workload, the ITTECF shortens ECF mentor training to one year and provides ready-to-use resources for additional support.

Considerations and potential challenges

While the ITTECF suggests an enhancement in teacher development entitlement, several considerations emerge when reflecting on how, and if, it will work better than its predecessor frameworks in practice:

- **Implementation challenges:** The transition to a combined framework may present logistical challenges for ITT providers and schools in aligning their existing programmes.
- **Balancing standardisation and flexibility:** It takes skill and understanding to create a balance between providing a consistent foundation for all teachers and allowing for adaptation to diverse educational contexts. This balance may be difficult to achieve given capacity issues evidenced in the previous frameworks (see chapter four).
- **Subject-specific development:** Although the framework is designed to be subject agnostic, ensuring adequate subject-specific development within this general framework may be challenging.
- **Long-term impact:** The effectiveness of this minimum entitlement for developing 'great teachers' will only become apparent over time, as the first cohorts progress through the new system. It will also be implemented without the support of funded NPQs to reinforce the 'golden thread' of continuing professional development for teachers.

The impact of the ITTECF on the quality of teaching (still to be measured by the government in relation to student achievement and progress) will be closely watched by educators and policymakers alike.

Conclusion

The Core Content Framework, Early Career Framework, national professional qualifications and ITTECF represent a comprehensive attempt by the government to develop and support 'great teachers' throughout their careers. These reforms reflect a policy shift towards a more structured, evidence-based approach to teacher development, with a focus on consistency and quality across the education system and fully controlled by the government.

However, while these frameworks provide a solid foundation for teacher development, they also raise important questions about what 'great teaching' means and how it can be cultivated. The prescriptive and outcomes-driven focus of the professional development reforms may risk oversimplifying the complex, context-dependent and intrinsic elements of effective teaching. There is a danger that in striving for consistency, these frameworks could stifle innovation and fail to adequately prepare teachers with skills that enable them to adapt to the diverse and changing contexts in which they work.

Furthermore, we have learned that the success of teacher development reforms in supporting 'great teachers' depends in no small part on their implementation. The increased workload associated with the CCF, ECF and NPQs served to undermine the effectiveness of the training and development (see chapter four). If not carefully managed, the ITTECF implementation may cause similar tensions in schools.

Ultimately, while the CCF, ECF and NPQs have provided a structured pathway for teacher development, they should be viewed as a foundation rather than a ceiling for entitlement. The ITTECF will be no different. Support for 'great teachers' should exceed the minimum entitlement, enabling teachers to flourish in the profession, with skills and understanding that allow them to continually reflect on and adapt their practice in response to the needs of their students and the changing educational landscape. The challenge for policymakers and educational leaders will be to ensure that the ITTECF and NPQs support and encourage this ongoing professional growth, rather than constrain it within rigid boundaries.

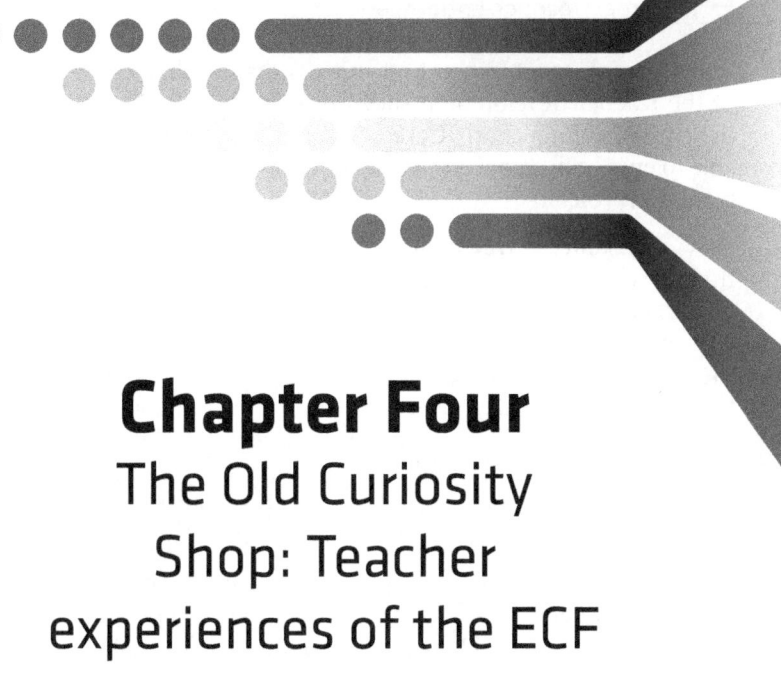

Chapter Four
The Old Curiosity Shop: Teacher experiences of the ECF

But now, all other considerations were lost in the new uncertainties and anxieties of their wild and wandering life.

Charles Dickens, *The Old Curiosity Shop* (1841, p. 32)

Introduction

Dickens's observations on human nature were often profound. In The Old Curiosity Shop (1841) we are reminded throughout of the value of what is lost, and the realisation of this is clear only when it is gone. Only a few decades ago teacher professional development was continuing, flexible and personalised, with continuing education and professional development (CEPD) supported for all teachers. ECTs may not realise the loss of this to the profession, but they will be embedded in the 'new uncertainties' of their new job as a teacher. Our hope is that by sharing their experiences of the teacher development they do have – the ECF – we can influence the path of the new Early Career Teacher Entitlement so that ECTs will be able to engage in career-long teacher entitlement that removes any anxiety from their role.

Previous chapters have explained how the ECF became mandatory for state-funded schools in England in September 2021, and that the ECF provided a nationally standardised programme of professional development for year one and two teachers. This chapter explores the experiences of ECTs, mentors and induction tutors who were engaged with the ECF from 2021 to 2023. We conducted primary research that enabled us to speak with 50 teachers (25 ECTs, 17 mentors and 8 induction tutors) about their expectations of the ECF and what their experience of the framework had really been like for them. All of the lead provider ECF programmes were represented in our sample of teacher experiences.

We found that the ECF was experienced by ECTs, mentors and induction tutors in different ways, but with expectations and perceived effectiveness being dependent for all teachers on the school context, support and opportunities for flexibility within the programme. Our research findings, based on the experiences of teachers who have had two years of engagement with the ECF, suggest that the programme only partially met the needs of ECTs, which could explain the sustained challenge that English schools are facing with ECT attrition. Mentors and induction tutors also told us of both good and bad experiences in delivering the requirements of the ECF. We are curious to find out, as the ITTECF unfolds, if it will mitigate the deficits found by ECTs, mentors and induction tutors in the first iteration of the ECF.

The research: why we listened to teachers' experiences

Our exploration of teachers' experiences of the ECF used a lens that positioned the ECF as a system with interacting elements across the full educational context (Arnold & Wade, 2015). The ECF system included ECTs, mentors, induction tutors and lead providers at the core of the system, but this core was influenced by (and influencing of) sub-systems containing individual, school and broader educational contexts, practices, relationships and requirements (see Figure 4 for a visual conceptualisation). Adopting an ECF system lens enabled us to appreciate the reciprocal influences of the elements and therefore the importance of listening to

Chapter Four: The Old Curiosity Shop

teachers' experiences of the ECF to establish a valid understanding of how it was working in practice.

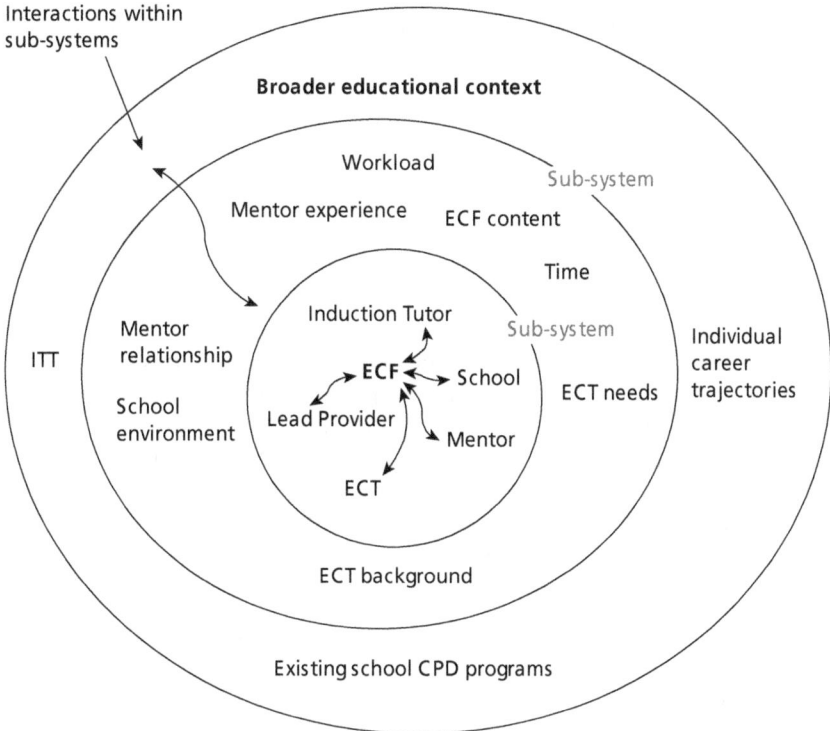

Figure 4: The ECF system conceptual model

Our research methodology

We used semi-structured interviews for our research, as we believed this method would give us data that would illuminate the expectations and experiences of ECTs, mentors and induction tutors. We interviewed the teachers who volunteered to take part in the research at the end of the second year of the ECF in 2023. The aim of our research was to capture authentic experiences of the ECF delivery and content across all lead provider programmes. We wanted to hear the voices of those who had engaged with it from the start until completion of the first cohort after two years (2021–2023) – the ECTs, mentors and induction tutors. Ethical approval was granted by both of our universities (Plymouth Marjon University and the University of Buckingham).

Semi-structured interviews were used as they supported the teachers in sharing their experiences of the ECF, with only small prompts from us to support the 'lifeworlds of participants' (Kvale, 1996, p. 30). The interviews were conducted using Microsoft Teams, a videoconferencing platform, to provide opportunity for any teacher to participate regardless of location in England. The interviews lasted up to one hour. All of the teachers were working either in a state-funded primary or secondary school.

We recognise that 50 teachers is a small sample of the ECF engaged population of teachers. At the time of the research in 2022, there were 47,605 ECTs and 11,445 mentors (Department for Education, 2022). However, there is a richness in the data collected that reaches across lead providers, phases and ECF roles and allows these 50 teachers' experiences to shine a light on ECF practices in schools. To contextualise our teachers' responses (and to fully understand the ECF system) we reviewed education policy documents, lead provider monitoring visit documents and all other relevant literature. This meant that when we read (and reread) our teachers' interview transcripts and listened to the recordings of the semi-structured interviews, we were able to fully 'understand, explain and interpret the phenomena in question' (Cohen et al., 2018, p. 643) from the perspective of the ECT, mentor or induction tutor.

When analysing the interview data we used an approach called thematic analysis (TA) (Braun & Clarke, 2022). We wanted to really listen to what the teachers had told us about their expectations of the ECF, and how these expectations had been met, or not, over the first two years of the ECF. Identifying themes in the ECTs', mentors' and induction tutors' experiences was a way of bringing the teachers' experiences of the ECF together as a system. The themes represent the features of the teachers' accounts that characterised their particular perceptions or experiences of the ECF.

Teachers' expectations and experiences of the ECF

There were similarities in the expectations of the ECF for the teachers we interviewed, regardless of their role in the ECF, the phase they were teaching or the lead provider being used to deliver the ECF programme. All teachers expected an entitlement to support in their role: ECTs through reduced teaching time and a mentor to support the development of their teaching, mentors through time allocated for mentoring, mentor training and resources to support them in their role, and induction tutors through time to support both ECTs and mentors in understanding the ECF and its requirements. These expectations were largely met by the ECF, with ECTs receiving mentor support and time, mentors receiving time with ECTs and opportunities for development, and induction tutors being provided with guidance on the ECF for implementation in their schools. This said, there were many expectations that were not met, particularly relating to quality of resources and capacity to engage with ECF roles.

ECTs' great expectations

Clear structure for development and training
A lot of ECF work   No repetition of ITT content
Advice and guidance from teachers in other school types   Regular meetings
Detailed support on how to develop as a teacher
Support network of other ECTs   Confidential space to talk
Support from mentor   Time off timetable for PPA
No tick-box learning
Mentor   Time off timetable for ECF   No offsite training
Two years of professional development and training support
Loads of support

There were also differences in experiences that related to school contexts as part of the broader ECF system, ECT differential learning needs and the level of mentor and induction tutor experience prior to taking on the ECF role. Experiences of the ECF were most effective when the mentor was experienced and able to adapt the ECF programmed flexibly to the ECT's needs. This also required a school context that had an induction tutor that trusted the mentor to support the ECT in achieving their two-year induction successfully.

Below we share ECT, mentor and induction tutor experiences as separate groups of teachers engaging and working differently within the ECF. We are mindful that ECTs have no choice in their professional development, that mentors have a range of training and experience of the mentoring role, and that induction tutors were introducing and overseeing a new framework within their schools at pace. This said, the contextual environment of the ECF system established similarities in experience that were in place throughout the research: engagement with a lead provider ECF programme, the provision of a dedicated mentor to support the ECT through the ECF, and funded time off timetabled teaching to do the work associated with the ECF.

Early career teachers' experiences of the ECF

> **What are the responsibilities of the ECT?**
>
> The ECT's responsibilities include:
> - providing evidence that they have QTS and are eligible to start induction
> - meeting with their induction tutor to discuss, agree and review priorities for their induction programme.
>
> Source: Department for Education (2025)

The 25 ECTs that spoke to us about their two years participating in the ECF consisted of 15 females and 10 males, and ranged in age from 21 to 32. The ECTs were from a selection of all school phases (primary to secondary) and all lead provider programmes (UCL – five ECTs, Ambition Institute – five ECTs, Teach First – six ECTs, Capita – three ECTs, Education Development Trust – three ECTs, Best Practice Network – three ECTs). Lead provider programme made no difference to how the ECTs interviewed experienced the ECF. The themes that emerged from the research reflect both benefits and challenges of the ECTs' ECF experience:

Benefits of the ECF

- Support from a mentor
- Time to build professional confidence
- Opportunities to learn from other teachers

Challenges of the ECF

- Overloaded with things to do
- Repetitive, generalised and ill-timed content
- Poor delivery of programme content

Benefits of the ECF to ECTs

Support from a mentor

Mentoring is clearly evidenced to have great potential in terms of benefiting beginning teachers in their professional development (Hobson et al., 2009). The ECTs we interviewed verified this, telling us that the mentors they worked with in school modelled great practice and offered continued support to them.

[I have a] brilliant relationship with my mentor. They are a positive person, with lots of experience and have been at the school a long time and know the systems. They are very supportive and give constructive feedback.

ECT

ECTs were positive about having a dedicated mentor to support them within the framework and felt that they had established effective relationships with them. They reported that the mentor support had been important to their progress throughout their first two years of teaching:

She [the mentor] is super helpful, really supportive and provides me with lots of new learning opportunities.

ECT

The mentor support was perceived by ECTs as being particularly effective when the mentor was either in the same subject area as them, or was confident in their mentor role and able to flex the ECF programme to the needs of the ECT and/or school context. This demonstrates that the success of the ECF is reliant as much on the relationship between the mentor and the ECT as it is on the content of the ECF programme.

My mentor is in the same subject area as me and has been teaching for a long time ... she can share her wealth of experience.

ECT

I struggled with the content [of the ECF] in the first year – it was too broad and wasn't specific enough for the early end of primary. My mentor gave me extra examples, which were great, as the ECF examples were not the language you could use with six- to seven-year-olds.

ECT

Time to build professional confidence

ECTs appreciated their entitlement to two years of support as a new teacher, telling us that it gave them time to consolidate learning and embed teaching skills. All 25 of the ECTs we spoke with had a better experience of the ECF in year two, having become more familiar with the content, process and terminology used. The familiarity with the ECF requirements led the majority of ECTs to share that they believed that their confidence in teaching and subject knowledge, and overall self-efficacy as a teacher, had improved over the two-year ECF period. The ability of the majority of ECTs to work with mentors to apply the ECF and explore new ideas grew by year two. The ECF programme provided useful tips, and sparked reflective conversations between ECTs and with their mentors.

I think I feel a lot more confident than I did at the start because I know what the framework looks like, and I know what's expected of me.

ECT

I think there's been a massive sort of increase in confidence and sort of knowledge and quality of the teaching that I'm delivering, because I just feel like I know a bit better and also the reasons behind doing it in a certain way. As well as, like, obviously through the readings and through the support of my mentor.

ECT

Effective mentoring and induction programmes have been found to contribute to increased teacher self-efficacy, job satisfaction and improved teaching skills over time (Ovenden-Hope et al., 2020). It is therefore not surprising that ECTs engaging with the ECF and developing a positive relationship with a dedicated mentor experienced a growth in confidence. The ECF provided the ECTs with an entitlement to a mentor which they realised supported confidence and growth as teachers.

I have had a massive increase in confidence and knowledge and quality of teaching, because I know more and the reasons for doing things from the readings.

ECT

Opportunities to learn from other teachers

We learn in the workplace by working with others who understand and can effectively do the job that we are learning (Eraut, 2007). The ECTs we spoke to suggested that this is correct, telling us that the most valuable learning on the ECF occurred through face-to-face opportunities to learn with other teachers, their mentor and by networking with other ECTs.

The ECF makes it feel like you belong to something. The face-to-face when it happened, meeting others, that's when I learned stuff.

ECT

The ECF programme provided formal learning opportunities aimed at enhancing ECTs' knowledge. The ECTs had mixed feelings towards the formal element of the learning, which included online lead provider-led training as well as face-to-face training. They enjoyed the ease of access with online delivery (no time-consuming travel involved), and the ability to revisit knowledge and skills development, but were critical of lead provider programme delivery style and content (see below).

When learning in a supportive professional environment, teachers' effectiveness has been shown to increase (Kraft, 2014). All the ECTs we interviewed voiced the benefit of the ECF being sustained over two years and in their growth as teachers being bound to the face-to face opportunities for learning from, and with, other teachers.

Two factors have enhanced my learning: mentor meetings and attending external training. Having a day off and liaising with other ECTs is good learning and mentally refreshing also.

ECT

Challenges of the ECF to ECTs

Overloaded with things to do

All ECTs interviewed struggled with the time allocated by the school to the ECF, even with the 10% timetable reduction in year one and the 5% reduction in year two. They felt that the allocated time given to ECTs for undertaking the ECF was spent on lesson planning, or being taken to cover absent teachers' lessons, rather than on engaging with the programme content. The demands of the school day meant that ECTs were missing reading ECF recommended literature and accessing lead provider platforms for resources, and were not watching recordings of lectures.

Pace of school was just too much that you don't have time in your breaks to access readings or materials.

ECT

[T]wo hours a fortnight isn't enough … people in teaching are going to burn out … [and] I am a career changer used to regularly working 60-hour weeks.

ECT

ECTs felt that they were experiencing capacity overload, which in turn caused them to approach much of the ECF as a 'tick-box exercise' to complete. ECTs may have reported growing in confidence as a teacher after two years, but in their first year as an ECT many told us that they had felt 'lonely', with flashbacks to their teacher training and feeling overburdened by the workload, and found the additional requirements of the ECF 'nerve-racking'.

The workload of teaching is emotionally super hard. I have found the routine stressful and overloading, and really struggled and not been happy.

ECT

I did the readings during term time and watched the videos, but I don't remember any of them because I was so tired. The job is so demanding, I felt I was there physically but not mentally.

ECT

The importance of ECTs being given time for their professional development has been recognised by the ECF, but the workload for beginning teachers is high and the ECF can feel like an additional pull on time. If it's a choice, ECTs will prioritise the time needed to enable them to teach their classes rather than develop their practice. The additional time expected of ECTs by the ECF is not equal to the time given to undertake it. The forthcoming review of the ECF by the Labour government should consider ECTs' capacity and consider realistic ways to reduce their workload to enable them to engage in both their teaching practice and professional learning and development.

From coming from the world of fashion, in education there seems a lot of unnecessary admin, and the inefficiency of systems is archaic in my opinion, and the yearly reviews. I've worked in the best companies in the world, which are forward-thinking, and the concept of filling out a four-page form that shows evidence that you've done your job is bonkers!

ECT

Repetitive, generalised and ill-timed content

All the ECTs we interviewed felt strongly that the content of the ECF in year one was generic and repetitive of the content delivered in initial teacher training. This ECT (and mentor and school) dissatisfaction with the content of the ECF is well recognised in the literature (Ford et al., 2022) and government (Department for Education, 2024a).

The genericness of it really hinders its purpose and you don't get anything out of it. So then it feels like an extra workload. We sit there and ponder, and then someone asks, 'Do you have a reflection journal?' I'm like, 'I haven't eaten all day.'

ECT

I felt the first year of the ECF was more repetitive with a lot of things already covered in your training year.

ECT

First year was repetitive of ITT year and not as good – it was not applied to practice, just one strategy loosely applied to another.

ECT

The ECTs we spoke to suggested that the sequencing of the sessions, as well as the content, was not appropriate to the specific needs of the ECTs. Learning and networking opportunities should be made more subject-specific and applied to specific teaching contexts. They also believed that the timing of sessions should not be prescribed, as they were out of sync with what ECTs were doing in real time in the classroom. The content was seen as too prescribed in terms of what had to be learned, but also too broad and lacking context (for ECT, phase, subject and school).

The 'one size fits all' approach of the ECF was believed not to support their progression.

Timings of the materials in year one were strange, e.g. structuring a curriculum in term two as ECT – why are we being dragged into a class and told to structure a curriculum when we are not even doing that? This should come at the end of the experience.

ECT

Poor delivery of programme content

ECTs felt that learning opportunities were hindered by provider training and the way in which the content of the ECF in training sessions were delivered. One ECT told us that the 'teaching' on the ECF was so poor they could literally see the transcript the facilitator was reading from. ECTs shared that the taught and online delivery of the ECF programme by lead provider partners did not model best practice and in some cases modelled unacceptable practice, with cognitive overload coming from an over-reliance on PowerPoint presentations that were read verbatim in taught sessions.

Way it [ECF taught session] was delivered, you wouldn't teach children like that – teacher was doing it so wrong. More like a lecture, with materials you need but you can't find and not structured or guided in what to do at all.

ECT

Death by PPT for training. 40 slides. Not effective CPD. If I was observed teaching like that I would get an inadequate.

ECT

ECTs told us, quite shockingly, that trainers were aware of the poor experience for ECTs but told ECTs they had no choice but to deliver in this way due to the large volume of content in each session. Several ECTs mentioned that the trainers lacked knowledge about what they were teaching and were unable to answer questions or therefore did not engage with the ECTs during the training.

Felt like I was in a cover lesson [the one-day workshop] – she was 'faking it til she made it'. She didn't understand the subject. Just reading through a slide show.

ECT

ECTs recognised the irony in their own training – they would not achieve final sign-off of their QTS if they taught their classes in the way they were being taught for the ECF programme. It is important to tailor content to individual teacher needs during teacher induction (Kerney, 2014). Some lead providers did adjust their approaches to content delivery in year two following year one reviews of their ECF programme (Department for Education, 2023), offering an explanation for increased satisfaction with ECF delivery for ECTs in year two.

Overview of ECTs' experiences of the ECF

Guidance was well received from the induction tutor, but even more so from a dedicated mentor who supported the ECT through the ECF programme. The role of the mentor can have a significant effect in supporting ECTs and on their retention in teaching (Murtagh et al., 2024).

ECTs felt that mentors within the same subject area, and with more experience as a mentor, contributed more to their teaching and learning development, as the ECF content, resources and delivery pattern could be adapted to their needs.

The two-year ECF programme period gave ECTs time to embed learning and build confidence and self-efficacy as teachers.

ECTs struggled with prescribed content that was repetitive of that used in teacher training courses, and delivered in a sequence out of line with their own professional needs and school context. ECTs valued face-to-face professional learning and development opportunities, particularly networking with other ECTs within the same subject area.

ECTs commented on their workload in school creating tensions for capacity overload when attempting to fully engage with the requirements of the ECF.

Mentors' experiences of the ECF

> **What is an ECT mentor?**
>
> An ECT mentor is an experienced teacher who is specifically assigned to support and guide an early career teacher (ECT), typically during their first few years of teaching, by providing professional coaching, feedback and guidance to help them develop their teaching skills and navigate the challenges of their new role within the Early Career Framework (ECF).
>
> **Key points about ECT mentors**
>
> - **Focus on early career teachers:** Their primary responsibility is to work with newly qualified teachers to ensure the school provides them with a high-quality induction programme.
> - **Instructional coaching:** They actively provide coaching and feedback on teaching practices through regular observations and meetings.
> - **Supporting development:** They help ECTs develop their skills in various areas, like classroom management, lesson planning, assessment and student engagement.
> - **Knowledge of the ECF:** They are familiar with the Early Career Framework and its components, tailoring their support accordingly.
> - **Professional relationship:** Building a strong professional relationship with the ECT is crucial for effective mentoring.
>
> Source: Adapted from Department for Education (2025)

A total of 17 ECT mentors spoke to us about their two years participating in the ECF. Ten of the mentors were female and seven male. The mentors ranged widely in age, from 28 to 67 years old. They were from a selection of all school phases (primary to secondary) and all lead provider programmes (UCL – three mentors, Ambition Institute – four mentors, Teach First – five mentors, Capita – two mentors, Education Development Trust – two mentors, Best Practice Network – one mentor). Lead provider programme and mentor sex made no difference to how the mentors interviewed experienced the ECF.

Chapter Four: The Old Curiosity Shop

Mentors' great expectations

Concentration on teacher standards
More structure Bigger and onerous workload
Great emphasis on subject   Opportunity to regularly see the ECT in practice
Use of research to inform practice and develop pedagogy
Tick-box assessment Overlap with ITT/PGCE year
Great depth of professional discussion Standardisation
Better support to ECTs due to longer period of time
Greater opportunities to support ECT

The age of the mentor did appear to align with their confidence as a mentor in that the older they were, the more experience they had as a teacher and mentor. The most experienced (and oldest) mentor shared that the role was a lot of work, and even harder for those doing it with less experience of mentoring:

It [the mentor role] could be seen as quite a lot of work, especially for someone who doesn't have a lot of experience, because they don't have the experience or knowledge to be able to pick and choose which bits you need to do.

Experienced mentor

Those new to the mentoring role (and the youngest mentors interviewed) were cautious and some said they felt 'anxious' at the start of the ECF, concerned that they were providing the right support and guidance to ECTs. One mentor new to mentoring at the start of the ECF told us that their confidence in supporting ECTs grew as they got to know the programme.

The things covered in the ECF are what I found out two to three years into my teaching, so my confidence with delivering the framework grew from there.

New mentor

The themes that emerged from the interviews with mentors reflect both the benefits and challenges that mentors experienced with the ECF:

Benefits of the ECF

- Supporting ECTs to improve practice
- Mentors' professional development
- Regularly talking and thinking about teaching

Challenges of the ECF

- Lack of context across the programme
- Poor programme structure, content and delivery
- Not enough time for the mentor role

Benefits of the ECF to mentors

Supporting ECTs to improve practice

All of the mentors that we spoke with understood that their key role was to provide support and development for ECTs. Mentors articulated that the two-year structure of the ECF, with state-funded time for mentor engagement with ECTs to support their completion of the ECF programme, did enable ECTs to improve their practice.

The two-year programme allows so much more support and will ultimately lead to better retention.

Mentor

Mentors spoke positively about the experiences of mentorship, accepting that the mentor role within the ECF has compliance requirements as well as responsibility for ECT support (Department for Education, 2021). The large majority of mentors welcomed the formalised role of the mentor within the ECF and saw the benefits of a structured programme with access to resources to support the ECT's professional development.

You're holding their hand and standing next to them to support them as they move forward and grow in their confidence, and the more their confidence grows, the less support and framework you need to put in place and the more it becomes a process where you're supporting their learning journey.

Mentor

Mentors' professional development

All the mentors we spoke with were interested in their own professional development, and felt that the ECF mentor role supported them in being up to date with current practice and was a benefit for their own teaching. They also shared that the ECF had made them more reflective in, and of, their own practice.

A massive positive in being involved in the ECF as a mentor is one's own professional development, because you can pinpoint areas where you can reflect that you are lacking and maybe weaker.

Mentor

The majority of mentors found being a mentor for the ECF rewarding because of the improvement they saw in their own teaching. Our finding echoes that of the DfE when it was reviewing the ECF and discovered that nearly half of all mentors undertook the role to improve their own teaching (Department for Education, 2024b). One of the mentors we interviewed summed up their intrinsic motivation for taking on the role:

I think it's an opportunity to stay ahead of your practice and continuously stay at the forefront of your practice, and just find out more exciting ways to deliver the curriculum.

Mentor

Regularly talking and thinking about teaching

The professional growth of both mentors and mentees has been evidenced to happen with structured and supported mentoring programmes through the experience of 'reciprocal learning' (Huling & Resta, 2001). The opportunity to speak regularly with a mentee – in this case an ECT – about all aspects of pedagogy and practice, and to think about what has been said and what could be said at the next mentoring meeting, can enhance and increase reflection on both mentor and mentee's teaching (Simpson et al., 2007).

The best thing about the ECF is having timetabled time to talk with your ECT.

Mentor

It [the ECF] has sparked more teaching conversations than I've ever had.

Mentor

The ECF is a complex system for those interacting with it, due to the way it connects with the sub-systems that support and work with it (see Figure 4) (Arnold & Wade, 2015). This complexity is evidenced by the mentors' perceived and experienced benefits of being part of the ECF – their role is to support and develop the ECTs they are mentoring, yet they also find the system supportive of their own professional development. Clearly the professional development of mentors in relation to their own practice, rather than as a mentor, is a positive yet plausibly unintended consequence of the ECF.

Guide for early career teacher mentors: contextualising and personalising Early Career Framework resources

Understanding the mentor's role

ECT mentors play a vital role in supporting ECTs through their two-year induction period. This responsibility extends beyond simply delivering standardised content; ECF resources must be contextualised and personalised to meet the specific needs of the ECT to be effective.

Strategies for contextualisation

1. Connect teaching to authentic experiences

    - Use real-world examples: Draw parallels between ECF content and real classroom situations your ECT may encounter.
    - Incorporate privileged testimonies: Share your own experiences or invite other experienced teachers to provide insights.
    - Make lessons significant: Relate ECF materials to the ECT's daily teaching life and challenges.

2. Align practices with teaching

    - Bridge theory and practice: Help ECTs understand how ECF concepts apply in their specific school context.

- Demonstrate practical applications: Show how theoretical knowledge from the ECF translates into effective teaching strategies (and provide alternative knowledge and strategies if these do not work).

3. Relate teaching to the ECT's understanding level

- Assess prior knowledge: Before diving into ECF content, gauge the ECT's current understanding and experience.
- Scaffold learning: Break down complex ECF concepts into manageable parts, building on what the ECT already knows.

Personalisation techniques

1. Know your ECT

- Conduct initial assessment: Understand your ECT's strengths, weaknesses and areas for development. Find out what motivates them as a teacher.
- Regular check-ins: Maintain ongoing dialogue to identify evolving needs and challenges.

2. Tailor support to individual needs

- Customise focus areas: Prioritise ECF elements that are most relevant to your ECT's current teaching context.
- Provide targeted resources: Offer additional materials or support in areas where your ECT needs more development.

3. Address specific contexts

- Consider school environment: Adapt ECF guidance to fit the unique culture and requirements of your ECT's school.
- Subject-specific application: Help ECTs apply general ECF principles to their specific subject area.
- Phase differences: Identify the specific ways the ECF requires adapting to support the phase the ECT is teaching, such as age-appropriate behaviour management, parent/carer communication, curriculum development.

Practical implementation

1. Collaborative planning
   - Work with your ECT to create personalised learning goals based on the ECF.
   - Jointly identify which ECF resources will be most beneficial and how to adapt them.
2. Reflective practice
   - Encourage your ECT to reflect on how ECF learning applies to their daily teaching.
   - Use these reflections to guide future mentoring sessions and resource selection.
3. Ongoing assessment
   - Regularly review your ECT's progress and adjust your approach as needed.
   - Use formative assessment techniques to gauge understanding and application of ECF concepts.

Overcoming challenges

- Time management: Help ECTs balance ECF requirements with teaching responsibilities.
- Contextual differences: Address any gaps between ECF theory and school-specific practices.
- Diverse learner needs: Support ECTs in adapting ECF principles for SEND or EAL pupils.

Challenges of the ECF for mentors

All of the mentors we interviewed about their experiences of the ECF reported experiencing challenges with the programme and how this affected their mentor role. Like the ECTs we spoke to, the mentors found year one to be more challenging than year two of the ECF. The key challenges identified by ECF mentors were very similar to those of the ECTs, focusing on poor contextualisation of the programme and inappropriate sequencing of the programme content, which was delivered ineffectively. Mentors also spoke about not having enough time to mentor in the way that they really wanted to.

Lack of context across the programme

All of the mentors we spoke with found some of the training from their lead provider difficult to relate back to their school context and to their ECT's ability. They all agreed that a more flexible model of the ECF, with 'pick and choose' modules would offer a more appropriate experience for the ECTs and their schools' contexts. All of the mentors interviewed commented that the content of the ECF also failed in its lack of context by subject and phase, or school. Their experience of the ECF's lack of contextualisation was that it forced them to adapt the content (and delivery pattern) according to the needs of their ECT and their school or MAT. This was easier for the experienced mentors to do than those new to the role.

The ECF is effectively someone giving you a lesson plan and the resources, and you modify it.

Mentor

In year one of the ECF a large majority of the mentors told us that they had not made changes to the content and process of the ECF, as it was a new, mandatory framework they had been told to support. This caused a great deal of frustration and concern for the mentors, as they were aware that this restricted opportunities for ECT development.

Online resources aren't reflective of the ECT you may have – you can't adjust the programme to reflect this, which makes for a poor experience [for the ECT].

Mentor

By year two the majority of mentors had developed more confidence in adapting the ECF content to integrate it with specific school and ECT needs.

The overly generic nature of it [the ECF] can seem clunky and inflexible. I add examples to show how it can be applied, with more subject-specific studies, as subject specificity is not there.

Mentor

All the mentors in our research suggested that a more contextualised ECF that could adapt to reflect school, phase, subject and ECT stage of learning would enhance the experience of the ECT at the beginning of their teaching career.

There needs to be a move to a more flexible model where you have a set of modules you've got to work through, but you choose which ones and how long you spend on them.

Mentor

Poor programme structure, content and delivery

All of the mentors interviewed agreed that the ECF was not challenging enough for ECTs due to the replication of content covered in initial teacher training programmes.

I think the first part of it is too didactic and basic. I don't think it's challenging enough. I think it's almost exactly replicating what was already covered in PGCE, without really adding another layer of challenge.

Mentor

They also told us that the ECF was poorly structured, in that the sequencing of sessions across the programme did not align with school or subject-specific delivery. Mentors felt that year one of the ECF had the potential to harm ECTs' confidence, not build it up.

Ensure the timing of delivery is in keeping with the school running it, so that it doesn't overwhelm the ECTs – got it wrong in year one. Content needs to be slimmed down too. The whole point [of the ECF] is to support not destroy them.

Mentor

Mentors felt that their role with their ECT was undermined by being told to support prescribed content delivered at specific times and in a specific way. A large number of mentors told us that that the ECF's structure and rigidity had impacted negatively on them, as well as their ECTs. This negative experience of the ECF structure, content and delivery was reflected by the ECTs (see above) and has been evidenced in recent literature evaluating the ECF (Murtagh et al., 2024; Ovenden-Hope & Kirkpatrick, 2024).

The majority of mentors were concerned that ECF tasks were a 'tick-box exercise' and required no real engagement with the ECF by the ECTs. By year two of the ECF, the ECTs we spoke to were fully aware of the weakness in the ECF 'assessment' of their progress, with many having found ways to circumvent the programme expectations, such as the ability of ECTs to 'tick a box' without completing the work required.

Online learning needs to be refined – watching a YouTube video for 45 mins isn't effective professional development. Have you watched this video – tick box – not good.

Mentor

Mentors shared that they were aware of ECTs avoiding tasks that they considered irrelevant, or that were out of context/pace with where they were in their development. In year one the majority of mentors picked up the ECTs for doing this, but by year two they were largely ignoring this activity, recognising that by avoiding ECF tasks considered unnecessary, ECTs were spending more time on tasks related to their practice. This conflict between ECF requirements and ECT needs demonstrates the chaos within the ECF system (Stacey, 1996) that mentors have been forced to navigate.

Not enough time for the mentor role

Throughout the chaos of the introduction of the ECF to schools in year one, and the subsequent embedding of the ECF in year two, mentors told us that they struggled to find time to engage with the materials that they were required to read to support the mentor meetings with ECTs.

Sometimes it's the hardest thing to try to find time to do the reading and the meeting.

Mentor

The majority of mentors told us that time out of teaching and allocated to the mentor role was essential for the success of the ECF.

Make sure that there is time allotted in schools so that the mentors and ECTs are supported to do it [the ECF] properly.

Mentor

However, in order to undertake the mentoring role effectively, mentors were clear that more time needed to be allocated to them. All reported exceeding the time given to them (and funded by the government) to engage with the mentoring role, but all felt it was necessary to ensure that the ECTs were supported effectively.

If you were doing it [mentoring] really rigidly, properly, you'd be spending five hours a week including the hour with your mentee. Minimum.

Mentor

The effectiveness of the ECF is influenced by larger systemic issues that exist for schools, such as workload and time constraints (Ovenden-Hope & Kirkpatrick, 2024). The large majority of mentors (and ECTs) reported that they had experienced issues with time and the requirements of the ECF. The funded time allowance was clearly appreciated by mentors and ECTs, but it was not sufficient in supporting them in engaging fully with the ECF.

Overview of mentors' experiences of the ECF

Mentors enjoyed supporting ECTs' development, and the more experienced mentors were able to adapt the content of the ECF by ECT, subject, phase or school, as needed. Those newer to mentoring were more rigid with the structure, sequence and content of the ECF. In year two the majority of mentors had improved confidence in their role in the ECF, and used more flexible approaches that integrated the ECT and their school's specific needs into the ECF.

Mentors were able to use their role in the ECF to impact their own professional development. Attending lead provider mentor training sessions and networking with other mentors enabled them to think and talk about pedagogy and practice, which supported them in developing their own practice. This aligns with the DfE report identifying that 46% of mentors undertook the ECF role to improve their own teaching (Department for Education, 2024).

The two-year structure of the ECF gave more time for development and for the ECT–mentor relationship to flourish. The funded time for mentor engagement was welcome, but was not enough for them to engage with their ECTs effectively. Additional time was used either for reading all of the materials provided by the lead provider or, for confident mentors, contextualising the structure and materials of the ECF to support more appropriate sequencing and resources that reflected the needs of the ECT by school, phase and subject.

Induction tutors' experiences of the ECF

What is an induction tutor?

An ECT induction tutor is a member of staff who coordinates and supports early career teachers (ECTs) during their induction programme. The induction tutor's role has different responsibilities to that of a mentor. Induction tutors are responsible for:

- programme coordination – putting the induction programme into action and ensuring it runs smoothly
- progress reviews – regularly reviewing the ECT's progress against the Teachers' Standards
- assessments – carrying out formal assessments at key points during the induction period
- supporting ECTs – providing support and guidance to help ECTs build their skills and knowledge
- protecting entitlements – ensuring that ECTs and their mentors receive their statutory entitlements.

ECT induction tutors are usually members of the senior leadership team.

Source: Adapted from Department for Education (2025)

The role of the induction tutor within the ECF was welcomed in schools, however there was some confusion and misunderstanding when distinguishing it from what the induction tutor role had been prior to the ECF. Induction tutors had acted as mentors to newly qualified teachers (NQTs), supporting them with a full induction programme (one year) to enable their progress towards full teaching status by ensuring they had met all of the Teachers' Standards. In the ECF, the mentor role was separated out from the induction tutor role (although in smaller schools the roles were found to merge) to enable the induction tutor to provide or coordinate the induction programme at school level.

Induction tutors' great expectations
Flexible and context-related content
The ECF to be used as a professional development mechanism
Increased autonomy of the mentor
Workload to be reduced from NQT induction   Time
Meeting needs of ECTs   Mentor CPD
Progression from year one to year two of the ECF for ECTs
Increased support post Covid-19
Variety in lead provider programmes

We interviewed eight induction tutors who were responsible for ECTs' progress towards fully qualified status over years one and two of the ECF. One of the induction tutors was male and seven were female, with an age range from 27 to 49 years old. All of the mentors we spoke with said they appreciated the additional layer of support the induction tutors provided for them to undertake their role effectively.

The induction tutors that we interviewed told us of similar experiences with the ECF to that of the mentors, and shared views of the ECF with both mentors and ECTs that were similarly positive and negative. The key areas induction tutors told us about were:

Benefits of the ECF

- High-quality mentoring
- Time for ECT professional development

- A culture of learning

Challenges of the ECF
- Generic, basic and poorly delivered content
- Time challenges for ECTs and mentors
- Increased workload for ECTs and mentors

Benefits of the ECF for induction tutors

High-quality mentoring

All the induction tutors told us that they thought the role of the mentor had more emphasis and autonomy within the ECF, and that it had illuminated mentor knowledge of the teaching standards and best practice, demonstrating the importance of mentoring for professional development (Thomas et al., 2019).

The ECF has raised the profile of high-quality mentoring and its significance … It has given new mentors a structured way to deliver mentor meetings and guidance.

Induction tutor

Time for ECT professional development

The induction tutors that we spoke with were still reflecting on the impact of the Covid-19 pandemic on their schools. The ECF was made statutory for schools in England in September 2021, which meant that mentors and induction tutors were supporting teachers who had trained during the pandemic and therefore had limited face-to-face teaching and classroom experience.

The induction tutors felt that the two-year duration of the ECF was beneficial in supporting ECT development, and that the mentoring role alongside that provided a well needed model of support for beginning teachers, as the first year of teaching is always 'fraught, rushed, stressful and anxious' (induction tutor). The additional year of support added through the ECF was considered to allow additional time for ECTs to settling in to the school, learn about classes and school routines, practices and policies alongside the pedagogy and practice. All of the induction tutors we spoke with believed in the importance of time for developing a full understanding of what it is to teach.

Knowledge of the teaching standards is essential [to an ECT] and it takes time to have a shared understanding of what these mean in practice.

Induction tutor

A culture of learning

With the ECF being used in some schools as a CPD programme, it could be classed as a professional development mechanism in its own right. Imagine the ECF as a library of professional development resources that is accessible to all teachers in all schools. The induction tutors considered the ECF in these terms and the staff involved with the ECF as professional learners engaging with professional development through their various roles in the ECF system. Again, the complexity of the ECF shines through for the impact it has beyond the development of ECTs. Induction tutors and mentors also benefit professionally from the model of development used for the ECF, engaging and enhancing their own practice through the learning they are supporting for the ECT.

The ECF is adult andragogy – you're a learner again.

Induction tutor

Several of the induction tutors told us that they felt the ECF had improved the 'culture of learning' in their schools, with all teachers on a 'professional development journey'.

The beauty that working in the ECF has is that every day I observe a new teacher and learn something new so I can go and try it in my teaching.

Induction tutor

Challenges of the ECF for induction tutors

Generic, basic and poorly delivered content

All the materials given to facilitators to deliver and train are homogeneous and generic.

Induction tutor

Similar to mentors, induction tutors told us that the content and delivery of the ECF was too basic for the differing needs of ECTs, and was repetitive of ITT programmes. The words 'generic' and 'basic' were used consistently by the induction tutors we spoke with. The need for flexibility within the ECF was mentioned many times across the interviews, as was the need for the ECF to be to be adapted to the school context and ECT needs. Induction tutors told us that there had been a decline in engagement with the ECF by ECTs in year two due to the generic, basic and poorly delivered content.

The onerous nature of the ECF makes it fell like you are teaching people to suck eggs.

Induction tutor

Training sessions for the ECF were referred to by induction tutors, mentors and ECTs alike as 'death by PowerPoint'. Induction tutors told us that they were 'given a set of slides to deliver which are crammed full of unnecessary and irrelevant information', and that they felt obliged to 'augment and contextualise delivery ... and pitch it appropriately for ECTs' in order for the content and delivery to be made engaging.

Time challenges for ECTs and mentors

All the induction tutors stated that time was a challenge for both ECTs and mentors engaged in the ECF. This corroborates the challenges with capacity experienced by mentors and ECTs identified above. Induction tutors told us that the requirements of the ECF were not realistic for the time commitment required of ECTs and mentors when considering the reality of teaching, particularly at the beginning of the career.

Induction tutors shared that ECT and mentor development was hindered by the additional time taken to access materials and review readings, especially at the start of year one when there were access problems on some lead provider platforms. School life expectations, such as covering lessons for absent colleagues, were not accurately reflected in the demands on both ECTs and mentors and the way this could remove time allocated for the ECF. Some induction leads felt that the ECF was 'an extra thing to put on the to do list' and 'time heavy', with some questioning whether there is a need for an induction programme at all if schools run their own programmes of professional development.

Increased workload for ECTs and mentors

Alongside the issue of time, there were strong feelings among induction tutors regarding the workload of the ECF. The high workload was considered a factor in the retention of ECTs.

More and more than ever, ECTs struggle and drop out mid-year. I am unsure if this is the impact of Covid or the significant increase in workload.

Induction tutor

Induction tutors felt that the ECF also generated work for mentors due to the preparation needed ahead of ECT meetings and the need to access lead provider platforms for the materials.

The ECF is a lot of work, a stupid amount of work. I see mentors re-teaching ECTs. There is limited mention of SEND, and materials are generic.

Induction tutor

A couple of the induction tutors we interviewed told us that the materials provided helped them to manage their workload, and were complimentary of the 'one-page summaries' that gave them the information they felt they needed to frame a 'concise conversation' with ECTs and mentors.

It is interesting to note that induction tutors used the same lead providers in their schools for the ECF as were already used for the national professional qualifications (NPQs). Induction tutors told us that this choice, to keep the same lead provider for all statutory CPD, was to embed a consistent whole-school culture of learning and the DfE's 'golden thread'.

Overview of induction tutors' experiences of the ECF

Induction tutors told us that the mentors benefited as much from the structured professional development offered by the ECF as did the ECTs. The large majority of induction tutors felt that the two-year duration of the ECF was beneficial in supporting ECT development and, alongside the mentoring role, provided a robust model of support. The induction tutors identified that the ECF supported a culture of learning in schools due to the way in which all staff with a role in the ECF were engaged in the professional development process.

The generic content of the ECF and its poor delivery were identified by induction tutors as a problem for ECT engagement. The government-prescribed content and pace of the introduction for the lead providers of the ECF programmes could explain this challenge (Ovenden-Hope, 2022). Concerns raised by induction tutors around the increased time and workloads for those involved with the ECF were also raised by teachers' unions, such as the National Association of Schoolmasters Union of Women Teachers (NASUWT, 2021). The time off timetable given to ECTs, mentors and induction tutors to undertake their roles was considered unrealistic given the requirements of the ECF, and the need to adapt materials for a more contextualised experience for the ECTs.

Teacher experience case study

Induction tutor: Henry Sauntson

I have been teaching since graduating with a PGCE in English and media in 2008. After working for a number of years as a standard 'classroom teacher' and middle leader I moved into leadership with a focus on teaching and learning, but also with a responsibility for the support of ITT and NQT (as it was then!). This unveiled a bit of a 'passion' for teacher development which, when combined with my enthusiasm for research and evidence-informed practice in education, led me down the route that led to me becoming a SCITT director, working with pre-service teachers and their mentors to design and deliver initial teacher education. Although my specialism as a teacher is in the secondary phase, I work with pre-service teachers across all key stages and subjects/specialisms.

In my additional role as assistant principal in my host school, I am also induction tutor – a role for which I have received formal training from the local awarding body as part of the ECF. I still maintain a teaching timetable, as I feel it would be disingenuous to tell others how to do a job that I didn't still have regular experience of myself!

I believe very firmly that teaching is a profession of individuals, working as a team – we need to promote professional identity and take a heterogeneous approach to the development of pedagogues to ensure that codified and generic frameworks can be sensitively contextualised across a myriad of settings and contexts.

The role of the designated induction lead was one that seemed a natural progression from my existing role as 'professional tutor', a term derived by the sector itself to give a title to the person who oversees new teachers in settings and monitors induction. The biggest adjustment was the shift from simply managing a process of induction through internal monitoring and annual reporting to the AB, to a more structured, formatted and externally resourced programme from the verified providers; to me the biggest challenge is, as outlined above, taking a generic and centralised set of materials and making them relevant to the specific settings and contexts in which they will be enacted.

Having worked with the ECF and CCF from the outset it was easier for me to acclimatise to the 'learn that' and 'learn how to' approach – declarative and procedural, essentially – and also to the use of an evidence base; a significant hurdle is the language of the framework and the alignment with existing practice in schools – there are no new ideas in teaching, apparently, but not everyone knows all the old ones! Terminology and concepts associated with cognitive science have proved to be unfamiliar to many more established practitioners acting as mentors, not because they are not effective teachers but because the 'why' behind their 'what' is either unfamiliar to them, or is referred to by another term. This calls for sensitive, empathetic handling of more experienced practitioners, without descending into patronising them or making them feel disenfranchised.

The role of induction lead is hugely enjoyable as it is so rich in both variety and opportunity. I am fortunate enough to facilitate ECF conferences for both ECTs and mentors in my region, and I always speak really highly about the benefits to my own practice that come from 'shepherding the calling of others' (Ayers, 1999); I learn so much from new teachers, and this makes me a better teacher too. Those going through the ECF after a high-quality ITE experience are the most evidence-informed, motivated and engaged members of staff, providing they acknowledge that they will always be learning –

no lesson plan survives its first encounter with a child, as we know; teaching is simply a set of predictions about what 'might' happen based on previous experience and evidence – no plan is ever a sacrosanct determinant of what 'will' happen, but the predictions become more and more like 'best bets' as we deepen that reservoir.

Humility and dialogue are essential to the framework in my view; an acknowledgement from all parties – ECTs, mentors, induction tutors – that it is a mutual learning experience framed in the dialogue of hope and belief in the ability to continually improve. There are over 180 statements in the ECF, and research indicates that the average classroom teacher makes upward of 1,500 decisions a day; they are some big numbers which can seem overwhelming unless the reality is created whereby it is OK to fail every day, in the sense that the next day we can be even better.

Reflection is vital – it can't change what happened yesterday but can improve tomorrow, and an understanding of effective and purposeful models of reflection that support and facilitate development as opposed to just enabling navel-gazing and retrospection are important tools to acquire in the early years of teaching.

Teaching is a complex, highly contingent profession, with decisions to be made constantly, depending on the immediate needs of the students in the classroom at the time; it cannot simply be reduced to a set of codified statements and a framework of competencies; it is far more than that. Competency as a teacher can take up to five years to acquire; we have to make sure that pre-service and early careers understand this, and don't try to be a world-standard decathlete before they can master the art of running 100m; we can't – and should not expect to be – good at everything; I know I'm not, and I don't mind sharing that!

Experience does not necessarily equate to expertise, so pre-service and early career teachers need to be exposed to numerous models and approaches – as well as the daily realities of the life of a teacher – so that when they make the transition from early idealism, which is built on their own experiences of school and teachers they admired and want to emulate, into the 'survival' phase, they can see that there is light at the end of the induction tunnel; their competencies will increase, thus boosting their confidence. They will learn the two 'eff' words teachers can promote – efficiency and effectiveness. Their reservoir of experience will deepen, and their repertoire of strategies will grow ever broader with each day in the classroom, and they will hopefully embrace continued development and avoid the stagnant trap of habituation; automaticity is indeed that double-edged sword. Mentors need training in supporting this thinking from their mentees, but they also need to help them become culturally aware, embrace an ethical approach to their work and – most importantly, I feel – develop a professional identity born out of their core purpose in becoming a teacher, their beliefs about education, and their values.

Recent reforms suggest that the sector is once again under scrutiny, which can only be a good thing in terms of focus and attention; however, I have learned through experience that the best thing anyone working within pre-service and early career teaching can be is responsive; mentors are teachers too, and need time to fulfil all aspects of their role effectively, as well as receiving the necessary training required to undertake their additional roles. There will, hopefully, be a chance to acknowledge the relevant prior learning and experience of mentors, but also to ensure that they have access to those essential networks that help build education as a collegiate profession. A school needs a culture of mentorship.

We must never assume that communication has taken place – sometimes this is illusory, hidden behind the frameworks that provide the vocabulary and structure for the supposed conversations and support for ECTs, and for mentors; we must not enter into a Tower of Babel situation where everyone talks in different tongues and ultimately fails to complete their intended aims – we need to acknowledge that the call to teach is the call to shepherd others – students or teachers. We have a chance to use our experience and knowledge to help novices get better, and in so doing ensure better outcomes for students – that's why the role of induction lead is so important.

I feel it is my duty, nay my imperative, to foster a sense of uniqueness and heterogeneity in the teachers with whom I work – they need to be reflective practitioners, with clear professional identities, ethical and

> moral imperatives, and a real reason to be a teacher, developed and honed through their increasing practice wisdom.
>
> Above all, they need to know not only what they are doing but why they are doing it. Teachers should be able to give a coherent justification for their practices citing (i) evidence, (ii) pedagogical principle and (iii) educational aim, rather than offering the unsafe defence of compliance. Anything else is educationally unsound and mere compliance is the defence of the oppressed.

Conclusion

The ECTs, mentors and induction tutors in our research reported both positive and negative experiences of the ECF. The positive experiences had enhanced their practice through new ideas, insights and relationships that had developed their self-confidence and self-efficacy as teachers and/or in their ECF role. The ECF system had connected these teachers with other teachers through the school sub-systems, such as classroom observations and mentor–ECT meetings, that support and form the ECF. These experiences met some of the great expectations held for the ECF by the ECTs, mentors and induction tutors.

Our teachers also shared their poor experiences of the ECF, such as the prescribed, basic and generic content of materials that were delivered poorly and without context, and the additional time and work beyond the allowance given for those participating in, and delivering the requirements of the ECF.

ECT, mentor and induction tutor shared experiences of the ECF

What the ECF does well	What the ECF does not do well
Time to build professional confidence and develop	Overloaded with things to do – not enough time
Opportunities to learn from other teachers – regularly talking and thinking about teaching	Repetitive, generic and ill-timed content – complete lack of context
Support to improve practice	Poor delivery of programme content
High-quality mentoring	Not enough time for the mentor role
A culture of learning	

The ECF was developed by the DfE to enhance professional development for beginning teachers, provide comprehensive support for ECTs over two years and thereby support ECT retention. The mentor role was enhanced through a formal mentoring programme within the ECF, dedicated mentor training, protected time for the mentor and clear mentor–ECT relationship expectations. The induction tutor role was separated from the mentor role to provide another layer of system support for the ECF and those engaged with it. The ECF is a significant school commitment, working within a broad educational system with existing competing demands on school and teacher capacity.

Teacher experiences have all been impacted by the ECF system interactions, which have resulted not only in the retention of the ECF for ECT induction but also in a full review by the DfE in 2024 to understand and mitigate the challenges experienced by those involved (Department for Education, 2024a). The DfE acknowledged under the Conservative government that a change to the ECF to align it more closely to the needs of ECTs and schools was required. The DfE announced a new framework, the Initial Teacher Training and Early Career Framework (ITTECF) (Department for Education, 2024b) to replace the ECF in schools from September 2025. Following the election of the Labour government in 2024, an announcement was made by the DfE in January 2025 that the ECF would be renamed the Early Career Teacher Entitlement (ECTE) and a full review of the ECF will take place in 2027. The ITTECF would still become the statutory provision for schools in September 2025 as planned. The changes introduced in September 2025 focus on improving 'mentor workload, flexibility, and contextualisation' (Department for Education, 2025), all areas of the ECF identified as challenging by our teachers. The changes to the ECF are discussed in detail in chapter five.

Chapter Five
Our Mutual Friend: The Initial Teacher Training and Early Career Framework (ITTECF)

Is it better to have had a good thing and lost it, or never to have had it?

Charles Dickens, *Our Mutual Friend* (1865, p. 361)

Introduction

The main themes from Dickens's novel *Our Mutual Friend* (1865) are used in this chapter to tell the story of the government teacher development reform, the Initial Teacher Training and Early Career Framework (ITTECF) (Department for Education, 2024b). The themes explored by Dickens align with the journey made in England to arrive at the ITTECF, which are 'rebirth', 'regeneration', 'education' and 'greed'. The concept of 'rebirth' is used to explore the origins of the ITTECF, while 'regeneration' considers the rationale behind the changes made to create a combined framework. 'Education' offered us a lens for comparing similar models of teacher development in international settings with the approach of the government in England to teacher development. Lastly, we use 'greed' as a tool for exploring the neoliberal ideology in government reform of teacher education, examining issues of control and prescription in the ITTECF.

Rebirth

The ITTECF has its roots in the Teacher Recruitment and Retention Strategy launched by the Department for Education in January 2019 (Department for Education, 2019). This strategy recognised the challenges in attracting and retaining teachers, particularly ECTs, and the issues caused by poor teacher supply. The original ECF, which became mandatory in September 2021 (Department for Education, 2019a), was part of this strategy and aimed to improve both teacher recruitment and retention through ECT entitlement to structured, statutory professional development, to allow ECTs to succeed at the start of their careers.

The Initial Teacher Training Core Content Framework (CCF) was first published in 2019 and defined the minimum entitlement for all trainee teachers (Department for Education, 2019) based on the 'best available evidence', setting out what ITT providers should use when designing their ITT programmes. The CCF supported and aligned with the ECF in creating an entitlement to a structured three-year support package for ECTs (one year CCF, two years ECF), with 'learn that' and 'learn how to' statements setting out what ECTs should know (Department for Education, 2019a).

Rationale for the development of the ITTECF

Repetitive ITT content

The ITTECF includes different wording on progression and provides ECTs with information about what knowledge and skills they should develop.

ECF providers to pitch content based on ECT prior knowledge from ITT.

Need for contextualisation to different settings and subjects

ECTs are able to link content to own subject area and context. Mentors will have tailored resources and subject-specific materials.

Support for teaching pupils with SEND

More detail added to content related to adaptive teaching and supporting pupils with SEND, adaptions made to NPQs for SENCOs. Statements have been amended to improve inclusivity for SEND.

Source: Bromley (2024)

The ITTECF (Department for Education, 2024b) is representative of a shift in teacher development policy in England. The framework, implemented in schools from September 2025, integrated the Initial Teacher Training Core Content Framework (CCF) and the Early Career Framework (ECF) into a single, cohesive framework. The intention was to create a more coherent pathway for beginning teachers (Department for Education, 2024d), to reduce the repetition of content that had been experienced by ECTs in the first rollout of the ECF (2021–2023) (see chapter four for the experiences of ECTs). Concerns over workload, lack of flexibility and context had been simmering around teacher training and development since the implementation of the ITT CCF in 2020 and the ECF in 2021 (Creagh et al., 2023; Cumiskey, 2024). Concerns were raised by school leaders, ECTs, ECT mentors and teacher education professional bodies, and lessons learned from the first years of CCF implementation and ECF delivery, about the similarities between and repetitive content of the ITT Core Content Framework (CCF) and the ECF (Department for Education, 2023a).

Changes have occurred based on a call for evidence (Department for Education, 2024d) by the DfE in 2023 on the CCF and ECF (Department for Education, 2023a), and the outcomes of the review of the evidence collected by the DfE were published in 2024 (Department for Education, 2024d). The combined framework for ITT and ECF, the ITTECF that included an updated evidence base, was announced in January 2024 (Department for Education, 2024b), for implementation in September 2025 (Department for Education, 2024e) in this updated version.

What is the ITTECF?

The ITTECF is part of government reform of teacher development in England, and was developed as a response to outcomes of a Department for Education review of existing Initial Teacher Training (ITT), its Core Content Framework (CCF) and the Early Career Framework (ECF) for early career teachers (ECTs) in 2024. The Initial Teacher Training Core Content Framework (CCF) and the Early Career Framework (ECF) were integrated to create the ITTECF as a single, cohesive framework intended to offer a streamlined, structured and evidence-based pathway of development and support for new teachers. Mandatory in schools from September 2025, the ITTECF provides a three-year teacher development entitlement for trainee teachers and ECTs.

The ITTECF combined framework was developed with the ambition of providing a high-quality training experience for teachers, to enable them to support the diverse needs of their students (Department for Education, 2024d). Additional content in the ITTECF for ECTs was hoped to be a way of increasing their confidence and decision-making as teachers (Department for Education, 2024d). The Education Endowment Foundation, advisor to the DfE on the content of teacher development reform, stated at the launch of the ITTECF that it would provide 'more granular detail than any preceding national policy, providing a common understanding of effective practice' (Madgwick, 2024, para. 1). However, as we explored in chapter three, the notion of effective practice is contentious and needs unpacking further to avoid an economistic, student achievement driver only, which may negatively impact on teachers' development. This said, the ITTECF does consider the progression of knowledge and skills for teachers from ITT to ECF, which is essential in supporting effective teacher development (see chapter three for a discussion on what effective teacher development may look like).

Regeneration

Changes made to the CCF and ECF were a response to the outcomes of the review in 2023 (Department for Education, 2023a) and published in 2024 (Department for Education, 2024d). The revised ITTECF (Department for Education, 2024b) emphasised progression of ECT knowledge and skills from ITT to ECF, with beginning teachers being given three years from training to teaching to embed these skills. The updated ECF element of the ITTECF was adapted to include teacher development on specific subjects and phases (Department for Education, 2024e), removing an element of the generic prescription in content identified by the teachers in our research (see chapter four) and in the DfE review findings (Department for Education, 2024d). The 50 teachers that we spoke to (see chapter four) reported that those ECT mentors that adapted the ECF content and resources by subject and age phase for their ECT provided a better experience for the ECT, which was believed to enhance their practice.

The Oak National Academy, an executive non-departmental public body sponsored by the DfE, which was developed with government funding during the Covid-19 pandemic to provide online resources to school teachers to support online teaching, was appointed to develop the subject-specific materials underpinning the ECF element of the ITTECF and assisted lead providers specifically with their programmes. Diagnostic testing was introduced into programmes to ensure ECTs could focus on areas of development rather than following irrelevant sequenced delivery that hindered learning. Providers had the opportunity to design their programmes to consider ECT prior knowledge and learning to pitch the programme according to needs. These changes were clear responses to the concerns raised on the lack of personalised learning opportunities for ECTs in the first ECF.

In policy documents for teacher development reform since 2019, such as Ofsted's independent review of teachers' professional development (Ofsted, 2021), the policy paper on delivering world-class teacher development (Department for Education, 2022c) and the report on effective professional development by the EEF (Education Endowment Foundation, 2021), it is evident that the mentor role was considered central to the ECF's success, with the government making investments in mentor training and time. But mentors found the role challenging due to the demands it placed on their time, particularly when they devised additional resources to contextualise their ECT's experiences (see chapter four for further information on mentor and ECT experiences of the ECF). Reducing mentor workload was therefore highlighted as a key priority in the revised framework. However, reviews of the ECF demonstrated that mentors needed increased autonomy, and in some cases further upskilling, to provide ECTs with a quality training experience (Murtagh et al., 2024). The government's approach to attempting to reduce mentors' workload was to:

- **Provide enhanced subject-specific materials developed by Oak National Academy** (see above).

- **Reduce mentor training from two years to one year.** Due to the reduction in length of mentor training, shorter training focused on aspects believed to be most valuable for developing the mentor role. It is interesting to note that, in 2024/25, lead providers were required to deliver 20 hours of mentor training and six hours of refresher training under the initial teacher training criteria. However, the demands of this ITT mentor training were found not only to increase the workload of mentors but also to keep them away from school for too long, causing challenges for teaching timetables in school. Just two months after its introduction, this approach to ITT mentor training was scrapped based on ITT providers' feedback.

- **Give lead providers responsibility for developing and delivering resources to mentors to support one-to-one mentoring sessions with ECTs** (ensuring the resources had the flexibility to focus on self-study areas relevant to the needs of the ECT). It was intended that schools and lead providers would take responsibility for appointing an additional ITT lead mentor role to support the quality of mentoring in practice. The DfE promised schools and accredited providers £25 million to pay for this role (Department for Education, 2024d). It was hoped that the additional funding would give mentors time off timetable to access 'high-quality' training. The ITTECF also provided additional consideration for ECT development, offering clear direction for supporting pupils with special educational needs and disabilities (SEND) (Department for Education, 2024d). Content was adapted, and resources and special needs exemplification materials were made available that were more relatable to teaching and supporting pupils with SEND. It also used improved resources on oracy, early cognitive development, and social and emotional learning in the framework.

The ITTECF enabled schools that chose to deliver their own ECT development and support programmes to engage with a far easier quality assurance process and to benefit from a reduction in administration charges compared to previous years.

What are the key features of the ITTECF?

Coherent progression from ITT to the ECF

Subject-specific and phase-specific resources

Resources designed by Oak National Academy

Diagnostic testing to focus on ECT developmental needs

Reduction in mentor workload and training

Emphasis on SEND

Updated evidence base

Source: Cumiskey (2024)

The ITTECF has had some positive responses from the education sector as a framework to improve teacher development (Gill, 2024). These positive responses, however, have been equally matched by great concerns. The evidence base that informs teacher development remains controlled (and some would say restricted) by the government (Martin, 2024). There are fears of Ofsted inspection issues when ITT providers have to demonstrate what is being delivered in ITT and what the ECF contribution is (Brooks, 2024). Separating out the two phases of beginning teacher training and development is challenged by having 'learn that' statements and evidence reference lists that are identical for both the CCF and the ECF. It is quite revealing to note that, when uploaded to plagiarism software copyleaks.com, there is an 84.2% match, with 68.4% identical text between both frameworks (Turvey, 2024).

The standardisation of content for trainee teachers and ECTs reduces opportunities for contextualisation in practice, which raises concerns of a 'monopolised narrative' (Turvey, 2024) in terms of what teachers should know in the first three years of teaching. It makes us feel that Dickens was right to critique an education system that teaches 'facts' at the expense of developing the mind. How can teachers develop a toolkit of strategies that they can adapt in practice if they are limited in their exposure to the range of possibilities? The ECTs we spoke with commented on the repetition in the ECF of content from their ITT programmes and the lack of progression of knowledge (see chapter four for more on this). The ITTECF applies the same concepts of working memory, long-term memory, retrieval practice and quizzing pupils for fluency that occur in the CCF and ECF. The risk of repetition in learning for ECTs therefore remains high. Even more challenging for the development of 'great teachers' is the notion of the 'best evidence', which is 'provided' to beginning teachers without reference to the concepts that teachers should know (Turvey, 2024).

> ## Teacher experience case study
>
> **Multi-academy trust ECT lead (induction tutor, mentor and lead for ECT development across all schools in the MAT): Hayley Bissenden**
>
> The role of trust lead for ECTs was introduced to our trust in 2022. At the time, I was working part-time as a teacher and professional tutor in a large secondary school, while also collaborating with a local teacher training provider. When the new changes were implemented, I became intrigued and approached our CEO with the idea of supporting all our schools to reduce duplication and workload. The CEO agreed to allocate me one day a week to develop this role. It has since evolved into a full-time position that now encompasses ITT and CPD across the trust.
>
> I believe my success in this role is largely due to my extensive experience in ITT, covering both primary and secondary education. Before taking on this position, I spent eight years working for a local SCITT and served as the professional tutor in a large secondary school. During the first year of this role, I also completed an NPQLTD [National Professional Qualification for Leading Teacher Development], which, while interesting, did not significantly impact my work. The most beneficial aspect of my training for this role has been my involvement with the appropriate body (AB), particularly in delivering ECT and ECT mentor seminars.
>
> Since starting my role, I have worked closely with our AB, facilitating for Teach First and the National Institute of Teaching (NIoT). This collaboration has provided me with valuable 'face time' with ECTs and mentors, and a deep understanding of the content delivered during the seminars. This insight has allowed me to engage in meaningful discussions with ECTs and mentors during school visits. Without this knowledge, much of what they learn could have remained inaccessible, or 'hostage', as it would be solely dependent on the facilitator's input. I wonder how other people in my role will know what their ECTs and

mentors are learning if they are not facilitators. You cannot access the materials unless you are a facilitator, as these materials are not shared with schools – therefore the self-directed study and seminars lose value and often do not align with whole-school priorities.

I did not have any specific expectations around the role; I pursued it because I genuinely believed I was the best person for the job, primarily because I already knew the ECTs from their time as trainees. This prior knowledge and the relationships I had built meant that no time was wasted in helping them make progress. I also understood what they needed from the start. For example, I ensured all ECTs began by sharing their ITT transition reports with their mentors. This gave mentors a clear understanding of their strengths and areas for development from September.

My insight into ITT also enabled me to tailor the CPD I provided. For instance, many trainees are kept away from Year 11 and Year 6 classes during their training due to the focus on assessment, which often makes assessment one of the highest-leverage areas for development in September. Similarly, adaptive teaching is a key focus because shallow subject knowledge can limit their ability to 'pivot' effectively during lessons. Having this knowledge allowed my ECTs to make quicker progress.

I absolutely love my role and feel incredibly fortunate to have it. ECTs are a joy to work with, and seeing school development through their lens is similar to viewing school through the perspective of a disadvantaged child. When school leaders make decisions and implement changes with ECTs in mind, it often results in policies and practices that are accessible to all staff. This approach has been especially valuable in refining behaviour policies. If a new ECT can effectively use the behaviour policy from September, it is fit for purpose; if they cannot, it is not. Using this lens has helped us adapt and improve our policies.

What is not working, however, is the ECF materials. They lack stretch and challenge and are overly repetitive. Some of my ECTs are already taking on additional responsibilities and need more targeted input. Mentor engagement is another area of concern; the materials do not give mentors enough purpose – we need to integrate the AB and the

ECF materials more, add value and action. I also worry about mentors who have completed their training but continue working with new ECTs without any further development. For some, bad habits have started to creep back in.

The digital platforms are also underutilised. Most of our schools use StepLab as a coaching platform, and it would be fantastic if the national providers adopted it or offered something similar nationally. For example, integrating StepLab with the ITT platform, Mosaic, would allow a mentor to access coaching records from ITT through to ECT, regardless of the school. This would make the coaching journey person-centred rather than provider-based, enhancing continuity and ownership of professional growth.

I am a mentor this year in addition to being ECT lead. This is because I teach business studies, and the ECT I am mentoring is teaching business but is qualified in PE. I stepped into the mentor role to help him develop his subject knowledge. This highlights an important point: our mentoring meetings are often dominated by discussions around subject knowledge, as this is his highest-leverage area. However, from my experience with other mentors, it can sometimes be more effective if the mentor is not from the same subject area. This prevents the focus from shifting too heavily towards subject knowledge, and ensures the interaction remains centred on teaching and learning. The ideal scenario is when the head of department provides the subject knowledge input, while the mentor focuses on teaching and learning strategies.

At the secondary level, mentoring generally works smoothly, as sessions are timetabled on both the mentor's and ECT's schedules. In primary schools, it can be more challenging, but often more effective, when the relationship works well. Smaller primary schools, however, struggle due to capacity issues, so I frequently step in to provide support. When a primary mentor–ECT relationship is strong and fully supported by the school, it outshines other set-ups. Primary schools often foster close-knit relationships and spend significant time working together, which allows for excellent support for ECTs. However, the intensity of the primary environment can make things very toxic if the relationship is not working well.

The mentor role is incredibly rewarding but is not suited to all skill sets. I enjoy supporting and seeing my ECT succeed, but it does require significant time, effort and nurturing. Unfortunately, I find that the ECF does not support the development of mentoring skills or provide mentors with feedback on their performance. There is a clear need for a framework to offer feedback to mentors and to gauge the impact of their mentoring.

Tracking seminar attendance is another challenge. As a facilitator, I can track attendance for year two ECTs, but I cannot do this for year one. Most schools are also not in a position to track this data, and it is only possible for me because of my role as a facilitator. Additionally, school leaders often have no insight into what mentors are learning through their training, which is a significant gap. Establishing better systems for feedback, attendance tracking and mentor development would greatly enhance the overall mentoring process.

I welcome the idea of a unified curriculum through the ITTECF and its role in helping with the transition from trainee to ECT. While I believe it may embed the narrative more quickly – potentially supporting the coaching process and improving how development points are communicated – I do not think it will significantly impact teacher retention. Teachers do not leave the profession because they are unaware of what they need to improve; they leave because they lack the support or the ability to make meaningful changes. A prime example of this is behaviour management.

One thing I have identified within the trust is that some schools are excellent 'starter schools' for ECTs because behaviour and routines are well established and consistently applied. These schools are ideal for new teachers, as they can focus on developing their pedagogy and subject knowledge without spending all their energy managing behaviour issues. ECTs in these environments make rapid progress.

We are now working on strategically moving some of the strong Year 3–4 teachers from these schools to others across the trust to provide targeted support and share best practices. This approach aims to strengthen behaviour management and routines in other schools, creating more supportive environments for both ECTs and established staff.

Education

No other country appears to have adopted a framework of teacher training and development from ITT to year two ECT that is centrally controlled by the government. There are some similarities evident in Australia, which developed a centralised curriculum framework for teacher education framework (Australian Government, 2022) similar to England's approach to the CCF, and in the United States the development of the Institute of Educational Sciences and What Works Centre established a model for selecting educational research for teaching that replicates a similar template to that of the Education Endowment Foundation (EEF) in England (Barrett & Hordern, 2021). Australia also has an institutionalised CPD system for teachers that works within a policy framework that established a regulatory body accountable for conducting teaching professional development (Abakah & Wellington, 2023).

There may not be anything quite like the ITTECF in other countries, but many places across the globe have implemented comprehensive approaches to teacher development that give their teachers an entitlement to professional development. This investment in teachers is considered the route to improving teaching quality, and in most cases follows the economistic view held by the UK government – that teacher development improves effective classroom practice, which is measured by improved student outcomes:

- **Singapore** provides a structured approach to teacher development funded by the government, which includes 100 hours of professional development annually for every teacher. Professional learning communities (PLCs) are established in schools and led by senior teachers, with weekly peer learning time built into the school day (Stewart, 2018).
- **Finland** and **Estonia** have a focus on high-quality initial teacher education (ITE), with less emphasis on centralised, ongoing professional development (Stewart, 2018).
- **New Zealand** gives structured support to ECTs, including 20% release time for new teachers and 10% for second-year teachers. Mentors are allocated time to support beginner teachers (Darling-Hammond et al., 2010).
- **South Korea** has an ongoing requirement for teachers to engage in professional development, with 90 hours of courses to be undertaken

every three years after the fourth year of teaching (Darling-Hammond et al., 2010).

- **Portugal** has established teacher development as both an entitlement and a duty for teachers. It aims to improve and update teachers' professional knowledge and competencies, as well as promote professional mobility. Teachers can attend CPD during non-teaching hours or, if necessary, during their teaching timetable, provided there is no disruption to their regular lessons (Eurydice, 2024).

- **South Africa** has the South African Council for Educators (SACE), which manages a continuing professional teacher development (CPTD) system. This national framework allows teachers to earn professional development points by participating in various endorsed activities. Teachers are expected to earn a minimum number of professional development points over a three-year cycle (Department of Education, 2006).

- **Ghana** does not have a comprehensive CPD entitlement for all teachers, but the government increased the CPD allowance for pre-tertiary school teachers (doubled for professional teachers) to support the aims of the government in encouraging teachers to pursue professional development opportunities (Arhinful, 2024).

The English model of professional development seems unique in its government-controlled attempt to create a 'golden thread of teacher development' that is structured from ITT through to early career development and beyond. It could be argued that it is because of the government control over education in England, and its national curriculum, that this type of reform for teacher education was possible. Other countries may be limited in the CPD options for teachers due to a lack of well-specified frameworks and resource constraints – implementing and managing CPD systems requires significant financial and administrative investment, which may be challenging for some countries to allocate. Different countries have diverse education systems and priorities, which also make it difficult to implement a standardised CPD entitlement across all contexts. And, in some countries, education reform must prioritise improving access or infrastructure over teacher professional development.

Carefully designed professional development opportunities with a focus on pupil outcomes have a significant impact on student achievement (Sutton Trust, 2011). There is a balance in this focus for policymakers, however, in that the teacher's own self-efficacy will need to be supported to influence retaining them in the profession (Ovenden-Hope et al., 2020). A country implementing high-quality CPD entitlements can expect to:

- improve the quality of teaching and learning
- enhance teachers' professional knowledge and competencies
- increase teacher job satisfaction and retention
- support the implementation of educational reforms and new teaching methodologies.

The English ITTECF vs the Singapore model of professional development

There are similarities and differences between the ITTECF in England and Singapore's model of teacher development. These are shared in the table below.

	ITTECF	Singapore model
Similarities	Structured approach to teacher professional development throughout career	
	Clear national vision of what it means to be a teacher, with Singapore using the Singapore Teaching Practice (STP) model and England the ITTECF (Davidson & Camp, 2024)	
Differences Professional development	Focus on ITT and early career development covering the first three or more years of a teacher's career (Department for Education, 2024b)	100 hours of PD annually for every teacher that is funded by the government (Niemtus, 2024; Menzies & Quilter-Pinner, 2023)
Government control	Less centralised, with a number of organisations involved in school leadership, including local authorities and multi-academy trusts (Davidson & Camp, 2024)	Centralised control, with the Ministry of Education, Academy of Singapore Teachers and National Institute of Education collaboratively developing the framework (Davidson & Camp, 2024)

	ITTECF	Singapore model
Implementation	Time off timetable and mentor support and meetings, two-year structured package (Department for Education, 2024b)	Weekly peer learning time integrated into the school day and PLCs in every school (Davidson & Camp, 2024)
Career focus	Focus on the three-year structured package of PD and less support for teachers following this (Menzies & Quilter-Pinner, 2023)	Emphasis on PD throughout a teacher's career (Niemtus, 2024)
Time	Following the early stages of teaching, no set hours of PD for teachers (Menzies & Quilter-Pinner, 2023; Niemtus, 2024)	100 hours of PD per year (Menzies & Quilter-Pinner, 2023)

In summary, while both countries have prioritised teacher development, the model devised by Singapore offers a more comprehensive, career-long entitlement – guaranteed time for professional development is built into school life. While the ITTECF attempts to support beginning teachers, by comparison with the Singaporean entitlement, it is a short snapshot of professional development that lacks the structured engagement with teaching as a community of learning, and the time to read, explore and reflect in order to evolve as a teacher.

Based on in the observations made in the table above, comparing England's and Singapore's approaches to teacher development, and what we can take from international education systems (Stewart, 2018), we offer some suggestions on what can be included in any revised ITTECF in anticipation of a Labour government review of the CCF alongside the ECF in 2027:

- time for professional development integrated into school life; examples include streamlining meetings and reduction of administrative tasks, to highlight a commitment to lifelong professional development and a reduction in one-off professional development days
- professional learning communities and opportunities for peer collaboration (team teaching, observations), which have been shown to increase teacher confidence and job satisfaction (OECD, 2014)

- expert colleagues to mentor/coach other teachers in leading professional learning
- encouraging teacher research.

The Labour government announced the renaming of the ECF to the Early Career Teacher Entitlement (ECTE) in January 2025 (Chantler-Hicks, 2025). The ECTE will continue to provide support and training for ECTs over a two-year period and will have similar features to the ECF, with a training programme, mentor support, dedicated off-timetable time for training, evidence base and mentoring activities, and reviews and assessments. The ECTE will run alongside the ITTECF in the same way as the ECF was intended to. The ITTECF acronym was not changed. The number of lead providers for teacher development dropped from six to five, with Best Practice Network no longer continuing as a government-accredited provider. Accredited government providers delivering the ECTE are Ambition Institute, Education Development Trust, Teach First, UCL Institute of Education and the National Institute of Teaching (all of which were previously accredited to deliver the ECF). In targeting ECTs' professional development entitlement, the DfE has committed to:

- a smoother and cheaper process for schools to choose to run their own training programme
- increased support for ECTs in special schools, with partnerships made with expert organisations
- tighter and more streamlined registration process to access the ECTE.

Greed

The ITTECF is a clear example of government control over education (Mutton et al., 2017) through the development of teachers from their training to professional formation. This is evident in both the control of content and control of procurements for providers. The ITTECF maintains the government-prescribed approach to pedagogy and practice that was in the CCF and ECF. The EEF remains the chief arbiter of providing the 'best available educational research' for the CCF and ECF (Department for Education, 2024d).

Despite small changes being made to the evidence base, criticisms of the evidence being mono focused on cognitive science at the expense of other approaches are far-reaching across the education sector (Brooks, 2024). This creates a hierarchy between the prescribed knowledge provided by the EEF, and raises questions about the experts involved, versus the working knowledge of everyday teachers (Hordern et al., 2024). The case studies throughout this book that share teacher experiences of the ECF give voice to those engaged with the ECTE, and what they say should inform the development of new frameworks intended to support teachers' professional development.

What is missing from the ITTECF content and delivery for effective teacher development?

- Clearer guidance on age phases and subject-specific support.
- Support for early years and SEND, with more content on adaptive teaching and supporting pupils with SEND.
- Diversity, equity, and inclusion. Changes made to statements within the framework to offer more inclusivity.
- Increased resources and adaptive teaching to assist with teaching pupils with English as an additional language (EAL).
- Mental health and wellbeing. Increased signposting for ECTs on strategies to reduce issues with mental health and to prioritise wellbeing.
- Reduction in workload for mentors, with improved resources to use with ECTs and reduced length of mentor training.
- Guidance on how to deliver the content, not just what to deliver (see Ovenden-Hope et al. (2020) for more on the importance of the how professional development is delivered).

Source: Cumiskey (2024)

Professional development continues to be controlled and standardised by the government, which uses market conditions of competition to procure cost-effective providers to implement policy reform (Ovenden-Hope & Kirkpatrick, 2025). This neoliberal approach to education as a 'market' resulted in a range of levels of experience in the lead providers of teacher education, from ITT through the aptly named ITT Market Review (Department for Education, 2021), to the ECF and NPQs. The ITTECF has retained providers of ITT and the ECF from the 2021 procurement process for the ECF and 2024 approval/reapproval of ITT providers, which at least offers some growth in knowledge and experience of teacher education for those providers new at that time.

We have positioned the ITTECF, and ECTE, in the teacher development reform that has been implemented in England since the Teacher Recruitment and Retention Strategy (Department for Education, 2019). We have done this purposely in order to critically evaluate the rationale for the ITTECF and ECTE, and thereby understand its potential for success in achieving better teacher recruitment and retention. The standardised approach, and development of common knowledge, articulated in the ITTECF is bound to the neoliberal ideology inherent in the Conservative government thinking that established the reform (Ovenden-Hope & Kirkpatrick, 2025).

The ITTECF and ECTE may offer a more contextualised opportunity for beginning teachers, but it is a product of greed: greed in the form of neoliberal performativity, of accountability and managerialism, and of the greatness of the market (Ball, 2003) underwriting the development, content and delivery. There is promise held in the Labour government 2027 ECF review, but until then the era in which this reform was effected impacts its possibilities for teacher transformation. Teacher training and development that emphasises the delivery of government-approved knowledge over personalised and contextualised professional development that is informed by wide-ranging evidence will reduce teacher autonomy, agency and self-efficacy.

Conclusion

So, 'Is it better to have had a good thing and lost it, or never to have had it?' (Dickens, *Our Mutual Friend*, 1865, p. 361). In chapter four we alluded to an England of only a few decades ago, when teachers were supported through CEPD to engage with areas of development relevant to their practice. We noted that our current ECTs will not be aware of that loss but that those of us with a lifetime of education service are acutely aware of the entitlements we once had, the effect that losing these has had on the profession. But having understood what could be for teacher development brings hope for what might be.

The ITTECF, at the very least, provides a pin in a map that guides the government towards a better ECTE. There is support and development in place for beginner teachers. Trainees and ECTs have mentors who support them in applying theory to practice, providing feedback to nurture and develop their skills. The importance of the mentor cannot be underestimated in the development of teachers, as it is this connection to being a teacher that will make sense of what is learned in their training and development sessions. The combining of frameworks brings a glimmer of optimism for better progression from ITT to ECT, with less repetition in the development of teachers' skills.

Whether the ITT and ECF as a combined framework are 'mutual friends' remains to be seen. England's approach to ECTE has been under scrutiny since the change of government in 2024. Much could be learned by the government from countries that invest in a sustained duration of entitlement for their teachers, with mechanisms and models that enable flexible knowledge and skills development within supportive school communities of practice. Consideration of career-long entitlement, not just ECTE, is essential if we are to imagine a future where teaching is in demand as a graduate career of choice.

Conclusion
The Chimes

But the bell had stopped, before a word was spoken.

Charles Dickens, *The Chimes* (1844, p. 7)

Introduction

This line from Charles Dickens's *The Chimes* (1844) offers insight into the power of silence and a feeling of what could have been. It is a reminder that we should seize every opportunity for real communication before it is too late. The intention of this book was to share our evidence-informed views of Early Career Teacher Entitlement (ECTE) through the voices of teachers engaged with ECT development, using examination of government policies and reforms, present and future, running along the 'golden thread' and with consideration of what effective professional development for quality teaching really means. We wanted to communicate the possibilities for ECTE, using what had come before to inform what could come in the future.

The conclusions drawn are that professional development for teachers is most effective when it is relevant, flexible, contextualised and sustained over time (Darling-Hammond et al., 2017; Education Endowment

Foundation, 2021). Time is important. Teachers need adequate time to learn, practise, implement and reflect upon new strategies to facilitate meaningful changes in their practice (Darling-Hammond et al., 2017). The process of professional development and growth takes time (Education Endowment Foundation, 2021). Time allows teachers to engage with interventions that build knowledge, motivation, skills and support opportunities for cycles of experimentation to repeat, reflect, refine and develop teaching techniques (Evidence Based Education, 2025).

The teacher development reforms embedded in the Teacher Recruitment and Retention Strategy (Department for Education, 2019) committed the government to a two-year induction programme for ECTs, an increase of one extra year's support, in its quest for 'great teachers'. The content and delivery, however, lacked flexibility and context, making it hard to adapt to phase and subject, and sequence, for many ECTs and mentors. The ITTECF offers a minimum of three years' training and support to beginning teachers, from training to ECT year two, with promises of increased flexibility and context-rich opportunities for ECTs (Department for Education, 2024b).

Enhancing Early Career Teacher Entitlement

Extending the duration of ECT professional development and support beyond two years, moving teacher development to a career-long entitlement, could deliver the improvements in teacher retention and recruitment that were being sought by the Teacher Recruitment and Retention Strategy back in 2019. Teachers make significant professional progress in their third to fifth years of teaching (Podolsky et al., 2019), suggesting that additional structured professional development during this period could strengthen teachers' practice and enhance their self-efficacy, a key determinant in retention (Ovenden-Hope et al., 2020). Removal of government funding for NPQs has reduced opportunity in schools for sustained professional development beyond the ECT phase.

Any extended and sustained framework of professional development should consist of key components evidenced for supporting effective ECT progression into years three to five and beyond. This new entitlement is imagined in the table below, 'Career-long teacher entitlement: a model for the future'. Chapter four demonstrated that the current ECF entitlement, while supportive of ECTs, particularly through the mentoring they receive, has not fully met the needs of the teacher, schools or the system. ECTs are still leaving the profession and trainee numbers remain critical (see chapter one). The 'golden thread of professional development' explored in chapter two requires more consideration of its stitching if it is to achieve the aims of the Recruitment and Retention Strategy (Department for Education, 2019).

Considerations for place-based equity and ECTE

The challenges faced by teachers in small, rural and coastal schools in accessing professional development support, particularly through the Early Career Framework (ECF) and Initial Teacher Training (ITT), are well documented in recent research and warrant consideration for equitable access to an ECTE (or career-long teacher entitlement). Teachers in rural and coastal areas often experience geographic isolation as part place-based educational isolation, which significantly impacts their access to professional development opportunities (Ovenden-Hope & Passy, 2019). Educational isolation for schools manifests in several ways, which in turn raise specific additional difficulties in attracting and retaining teachers:

- limited access to resources and collaborative networks
- reduced opportunities for face-to-face training sessions.

Digital connectivity, including unreliable internet access, can be a place-based infrastructural challenge and a significant barrier for rural teachers seeking to engage in online professional development activities (Eghbal et al., 2020). This digital divide can limit access to virtual training sessions, online resources and collaborative platforms that are increasingly central to modern professional development initiatives. The financial and time constraints imposed on rural and coastal schools and small schools by tighter budgets can limit their ability to fund professional development activities (Ovenden-Hope, 2024).

Any equitable ECTE must recognise and mitigate place-based challenges for teacher development. Teachers in 'educationally isolated' school may face greater time constraints than teachers in urban schools due to longer travel times to attend training sessions, or the need to take on multiple roles within their small schools (Ovenden-Hope & Passy, 2019). The unique cultural context of rural and coastal communities can sometimes create barriers to implementing standardised professional development programmes (Heeralal, 2014), which are hard to apply in the contexts they are received. This suggests that tailored approaches that consider local needs and perspectives are required rather than generic frameworks.

Government investment in improved internet connectivity and digital resources for rural and coastal communities can significantly enhance access to online professional development opportunities (House of Lords, 2019) and will be required if any ECTE is to be equitable. The rapid expansion of digital technologies and the lessons learned from remote teaching during the Covid-19 pandemic may be changing the landscape of professional development access, but only if digital connectivity exists in that location. Implementing flexible delivery models for professional development, such as blended learning approaches or asynchronous online courses, can help accommodate the time and travel constraints faced by rural and coastal teachers accessing professional development (Luo et al., 2022). Targeted policy interventions, such as additional funding for rural and coastal schools, or incentives for experienced teachers to work in these areas, can help address systemic challenges (Ovenden-Hope et al., 2018).

Addressing these place-based challenges for an equitable teacher entitlement requires a comprehensive approach that combines targeted policy interventions and investment in digital infrastructure. The government's review of the ECF, and subsequent merging of frameworks with ITT as the ITTECF in 2025, resulted in a three-year training and development entitlement that appears to address some of the concerns raised for the effectiveness of the ECF (see chapter five). However, for 'great teachers' to be the norm in England's schools (see chapter three) the entitlement they have at the beginning of their career should be a career-long teacher entitlement, like most other professions, and equitably accessible.

The Education Policy Institute reported in 2021 that giving teachers a formal career-long entitlement to 35 hours of high-quality continuing professional development a year would cost the government less than 1% of total school expenditure and has been shown to bring significant returns for pupil attainment, with 'an average effect size equivalent to one month of extra learning for pupils' (Van den Brande & Zuccollo, 2021, p. 6).

Our hope is that the promised government review of the ECF in 2027 will take its time and seize the moment not only to reform ECTE but also to legislate for entitlement for all teachers – that it will also consider removing the current transactional framework for ECTE and move to an offer of time for teachers to develop their skills in, and then engage in, evidence-based enquiry. We currently have frameworks for teacher development filled with content that teachers feel they have to get through before they can get back to the classroom and do their real job. Add to this that secondary teachers in England spend fewer hours a year on professional development compared to other OECD nations (Van den Brande & Zuccollo, 2021) and the need for change is clear.

A teacher entitlement to continuing professional development and learning (CPDL) that supports teachers in being curious, collaborative and engaged in their own progression, as well as the school and system needs, has the potential to change teaching as a profession:

High-quality CPD for teachers has an estimated benefit an order of magnitude greater than the estimated cost, which indicates we can be confident that a well-implemented policy [for CPD entitlement] would have social benefits.

Van den Brande & Zuccollo (2021, p. 6)

Components of an effective Early Career Teacher Entitlement: a model for the future

An effective ECTE should consider the components shown in the table below.

Career-long teacher entitlement: a model for the future

Component	Description
Duration	Funded professional development support for ECTs for two years (which extends into a career-long teacher entitlement).
Mentoring	High-quality trained mentors providing regular one-to-one support (which extends into coaching through the career).
Reduced timetable	One day a week in year one, and half a day in year two for ECTs as protected time for professional development activities (extending to a career-long minimum of 35 hours per year).
Structured learning	Structured skills development for evidence and evidence-based enquiry to develop CPDL for knowledge and understanding of a range of pedagogical perspectives; teaching and learning strategies; subject content; student needs. Access to a full set of resources, including online journals/research. Develop teachers' skills to make career-long enquiries to support best practice for the learning context.
Observation and feedback	Regular opportunities to observe experienced teachers and peers, and to receive observations of practice. Time to apply learning from observations to practice.

Component	Description
Networking and collaboration	Facilitated peer support and learning communities.
Personalisation	Focus on individual teacher development.
Assessment	Formative assessment in school aligned with Teachers' Standards.

To conclude our discussion on teacher professional development in England, and ECTE in particular, we offer you a story of Dickensian persuasion to suggest a future where teacher development reforms have been far-reaching and teacher entitlement has established teaching as a high-status graduate career of choice.

Great expectations of entitlement: a tale of teacher enrichment

In the bustling metropolis of New Kernow, where the gleaming spires of progress pierced the ever-present fog, a revolution in education was quietly unfolding. It was the year 2035, and the teaching profession had undergone a remarkable transformation, guided by the wisdom learned from past reforms and a deep understanding of how truly to support great teachers. Gone were the days of overworked, underappreciated pedagogues struggling to keep their heads above water in their first years of service. In their place stood a new breed of educator: confident, enthusiastic and armed with an arsenal of cutting-edge teaching techniques.

Our tale begins with young Educator Ivy Naismith, a bright-eyed early career teacher embarking on her second year at Gargery Academy. As she strode purposefully through the school's hallowed halls, her footsteps echoing with the promise of a new day, she could not help but reflect on the personalised development journey that had brought her such professional growth. There was no single 'golden thread' of learning that had guided her on this path, but a robust array of learning choices, guided by her mentor, to secure the knowledge and skills she needed.

'Good morning, Educator Naismith!' chirped Dr Hope, the jovial Principal, as he bustled past with an armful of holographic resources for students and staff alike. 'Ready for another day of enlightenment?'

Ivy beamed, her face aglow with the fervour of one who has found their true professional career. 'Indeed I am, Doctor! And tomorrow, I shall be attending the Symposium on Adaptive Learning Techniques. I can scarcely contain my excitement!'

Dr Hope's eyes twinkled with approval. 'Splendid, my worthy colleague! How fortunate we are to live in an age where such opportunities abound for our fledgling educators.'

As Ivy continued on her way, she wondered at the change that had come over the teaching profession in recent years. No longer were early career teachers left to flounder in a sea of uncertainty, submerged in standardised readings of little relevance or help. She remembered her parents discussing with horror how teachers were disappearing, drowning in the quagmire of endless accountability and formulaic frameworks for development. Now, teachers were afforded the luxury of time – one full day each week devoted solely to their professional development for three full years, and an entitlement to one half day for the rest of their careers. This revolutionary approach had its roots in research demonstrating the profound impact of high-quality professional development on both teacher retention and student outcomes

This revolutionary approach to teacher development had its roots in the mid-2020s, when researchers had conclusively demonstrated the profound impact of high-quality professional development on both teacher retention and student outcomes. The government, in a rare moment of foresight, had seized upon these findings and implemented a sweeping reform of teacher training, development and support. This reform returned our noble educators to a position of autonomy, and with agency not seen for many decades.

Ivy's mind wandered to her dear friend and fellow early career teacher, Oliver Twitch, who was currently ensconced in the Virtual Reality Teaching Laboratory at the nearby Dickens Institute. There, he was honing his skills in behaviour management through immersive simulations, guided by the gentle hand of an experienced mentor.

As she entered her classroom, Ivy was greeted by the eager faces of her students (those present both in physicality and in holographic form). Young Timothy Patchett, a precocious lad with a penchant for mathematics, piped up, 'Educator Naismith, will you tell us about your learning day tomorrow? What wonders of pedagogy will you uncover?'

Ivy laughed, her heart swelling with pride at her students' genuine interest in her professional growth. 'Well, Timothy, I shall be delving into the intricacies of adaptive learning techniques. It's a fascinating field that allows us to tailor our teaching to each student's individual needs and learning styles.'

The class collectively 'oohed' and 'aahed', their young minds already imagining the possibilities. Ivy marvelled at how her own enthusiasm for learning had infected her charges, creating a virtuous cycle of curiosity and growth.

As the lesson progressed, Ivy deftly employed the cooperative learning strategies she had mastered during her first year of teaching, helped in no small amount by the observations of other educators in schools across the wondrous city, and through reflections on and in action in her beloved Gargery Academy. The classroom hummed with the energy of engaged minds as students worked together to solve complex problems, each contributing their own unique strengths to the collective effort.

Later that evening, Ivy sat at home reviewing her lesson plans, developed collaboratively with her peers at the Academy, reflecting on the wondrous support for her becoming Educator Naismith. The flexible, personalised and context-relevant development plan for her professional journey that would sit so closely with her throughout her career had already equipped her with a vast array of teaching tools, and had also instilled in her a deep sense of confidence and self-efficacy.

She thought back to her university days when teaching had been but one of many high-status career options she had considered. Now, she could not imagine doing anything else. Her chosen profession was so respected, so intellectually stimulating, that it attracted the brightest minds from all walks of life. She appreciated the privilege it was to be an educator in England.

Conclusion: The Chimes

A gentle knock at the door roused Ivy from her reverie. It was her mentor, the venerable Professor Havergo, who had guided her through the intricacies of the teaching profession with wisdom and patience, and challenges to stimulate the mind.

'Good evening, my Educator apprentice,' Professor Havergo said warmly as she entered, 'I thought I might find you preparing for tomorrow's symposium. Tell me, how are you feeling about your teaching so far?'

Ivy's eyes shone with gratitude. 'Oh, Professor Havergo, I am so delighted by my own learning journey and the impact it has had on my students' progress! When I think back to my first day in the classroom, I had high expectations of my personal development plan, which shone with opportunity like a light dancing on the leaves of a tree. And I have not been disappointed. The bespoke training and opportunities to think and apply evidence to my practice for the benefit of my students makes me feel on top of the world!'

Professor Havergo nodded approvingly, recognising the fruit of her work with the government a decade earlier to change the way teacher professional development entitlement was perceived and supported. 'That is precisely what we hoped to achieve with this new approach to early career teacher entitlement. By focusing on pedagogy, and providing ample time for reflection and growth, we knew we could support a generation of teachers who would not merely survive in the classroom, but thrive and flourish.'

As they continued their discussion late into the night, Ivy felt a profound sense of belonging. She was part of something greater than herself – a community of lifelong learning educators, dedicated to unlocking the potential of all students.

The next morning, as Ivy made her way to the Symposium on Adaptive Learning Techniques, she could not help but notice the spring in her step and the lightness in her heart. Ivy reflected on her growth as a teacher, embracing the knowledge that it was a continuous journey, not a destination. The streets of New Kernow were alive with the chatter of early career teachers from all corners of the city, each eagerly anticipating a day of intellectual stimulation and professional growth.

The symposium itself was a marvel of modern educational technology. Holographic presenters shared innovative research findings from across the globe. Delegates present in person and via hologram, to support accessibility for colleagues not in the big city, engaged collaboratively in interactive workshops, supporting an immediate application of their newfound knowledge to simulated practice. Ivy found herself engrossed in a session on neurodiversity and personalised learning, her mind alight with possibilities for her own classroom.

During a break, she encountered her old university classmate, Daniel Copperfield, who had initially chosen a career in finance but had recently made the switch to teaching, recognising that being an educator was not only high-status but also an incredibly rewarding career.

'Ivy, my graduate friend!' Daniel exclaimed, his face blazing with enthusiasm, 'Can you believe the opportunities we have as teachers? When I was in the world of high finance, I never imagined I could find such fulfilment in my work. But here, every day brings new challenges and rewards.'

Ivy nodded in agreement. 'It's truly remarkable, is it not? And to think, this is just the beginning of our careers. We have a lifetime of learning ahead of us. I really cannot wait!'

As the day drew to a close, Ivy found her sense of purpose sustained and nourished. The knowledge she had gained, the connections she had made – all of it would serve to enrich her teaching and, by extension, the lives of her students. She understood now more than ever that being a teacher was not just about knowledge, but about capacity to grow, adapt and continually refine one's practice.

Returning to Gargery Academy the following day, Ivy was eager to put her new insights into practice. She had devised a lesson plan during the symposium that incorporated adaptive learning techniques, allowing each student to progress at their own pace while still fostering a sense of community within the classroom.

As she watched young Timothy master a particularly challenging concept, her face beaming with pride in her student's accomplishment,

Conclusion: The Chimes

Ivy felt a surge of emotion. To improve outcomes for all children through teaching that she could adapt to their learning needs was a skill she knew she now had. This, she realised, was why she had chosen teaching as her career. Teachers had such excellent support to nurture every child's potential and facilitate their growth – it was a privilege beyond measure.

The weeks and months that followed saw Ivy and her fellow early career teachers flourish under the new teacher development entitlement they cherished so dearly. Each professional development day brought fresh evidence-informed insights and skills, which they eagerly incorporated into their teaching practice. The impact on their students was profound, with engagement and achievement levels soaring to unprecedented heights.

Word of the success of New Kernow's educational revolution spread far and wide. Collaboration was the key, with professional development shared globally from the outset – place presented no barrier to engagement or support. It was a new time for the teaching profession, with all marvelling at the confidence and skills of teachers from the beginning of their careers.

At the annual Educators' Gala – a grand affair that celebrated the achievements of teachers across the New Kernow – Ivy was surprised to hear her name called from the stage. Dr Hope, his face red with anticipation, announced, 'For outstanding contribution to pedagogical innovation and student engagement, we are pleased to present the Dickens Award for Excellence in Early Career Teaching to Educator ... Ivy Naismith!'

As she accepted the award to thunderous applause, Ivy felt a profound sense of gratitude. She thought of all those who had supported her from trainee teacher to second-year early career teacher: her mentor, Professor Havergo; her colleagues; and the visionaries who had fought to implement the revolutionary approach to teacher development that had benefited her so greatly.

In her acceptance speech, Ivy spoke passionately about the transformation of teacher development entitlement that she had been a part of: 'We stand at the dawn of a new era in education,' she declared, her voice ringing with conviction, 'an era where teachers are valued not just for what they know, but for their capacity to grow and adapt. Where the science and art of teaching combine and are recognised in a lifelong journey of discovery and refinement.'

She paused, her eyes scanning the room filled with fellow educators, all united in their commitment to opening young minds. 'But most importantly,' she continued, 'we have created a profession that nurtures the soul as much as it challenges the intellect. A profession that attracts the brightest minds and the most motivated hearts. A profession that holds the key to our collective future.'

As Ivy concluded her speech to resounding cheers, she knew in her heart that she had chosen the right career. The path ahead was long, and undoubtedly filled with challenges, but she faced it with unwavering confidence and boundless enthusiasm. She knew this because she had not been trained to teach, she had been developed – shaped by experience, supported by research and driven by a passion for learning that would inspire generations to come.

And so, dear reader, we leave our hero at the threshold of a bright and promising future. A future where teaching is not simply a job, but a professional, high-status career. A future where educators are empowered to reach their full potential, and in doing so, unlock the potential of every child they teach.

In this brave new world of education, the words of Charles Dickens himself seem particularly apt: 'No one is useless in this world who lightens the burdens of another.' And what greater burden can be lightened than that of ignorance? What greater gift can be given than the key to knowledge and understanding?

As the sun sets on New Kernow, casting long shadows across the bustling streets, we can rest assured that in classrooms across the city, dedicated teachers like Ivy Naismith are preparing for another day of wonder and discovery. For in this enlightened age, every day is an opportunity to learn, to grow and to shape the future – one eager mind at a time.

Afterword
By Professor Sonia Blandford

My meaning simply is, that whatever I have tried to do in life, I have tried with all my heart to do well; that whatever I have devoted myself to, I have devoted myself to completely; that in great aims and in small, I have always been thoroughly in earnest.

Charles Dickens, David Copperfield (1850, p. 610)

It is hard work learning to be a teacher. It takes no small amount of devotion to develop the skills, knowledge and understanding required. The challenge of recruiting, training and retaining the number teachers needed for all schools across England and Wales is not new. This book by Ovenden-Hope and Kirkpatrick addresses the main issues with creativity, insight and a profound sense of engagement in finding a solution to this perennial problem.

In brief, pupil teachers in the majority of schools were replaced by qualified, certified teachers in 1946. This was 50 years after post-graduate certificate programmes had been introduced for grammar schoolteachers. The number of teachers needed far exceeded the number recruited. Eleven groups of training colleges were established across the country, delivering programmes that led to recognised standards required for all teachers – these were not dissimilar to the current Teachers' Standards.

By 1951, 25,000 students were training to be teachers, more than twice as many as in 1939, but even this was not enough to fulfil demand. It was not until the 1960s that university teacher education programmes were delivered at degree level. This was a significant step forward for the profession, reflected in a major growth in applications. In the 1970s, only one in 12 applicants were accepted onto teacher training programmes. Clearly, university status was deemed relevant to the profession. Master's programmes followed, retaining and training future leaders.

The late 1980s saw teacher retention once again become an issue. The Education Reform Act 1988 aimed at addressing several of the underlying factors, including the introduction of 'Baker Days', compulsory in-service training for teachers. At the time, the focus was on the introduction of the national curriculum, which led to a further increase in the number of teachers leaving the profession – curriculum and assessment workload have remained problematic for all teachers.

The government legislated for the Teacher Training Agency in 1994 to be responsible for initial and continuing professional development. Teacher and leader qualifications were framed by what was known as the 'Rainbow Pack'. National professional qualifications for head teachers and middle leaders followed, with universities commissioned to deliver a curriculum with generic resources. National professional qualifications were mandatory for head teachers from 1998 to 2012. Further changes to initial and teacher continuing professional development were led by the merger in 2013 of the Teacher Development Agency (reconstituted from the Teacher Training Agency in 2005) and the National College for School Leadership (formed in 2012) to create the National College for Teaching and Leadership (NCTL). By 2018 the NCTL had closed.

Teacher recruitment, training and retention in the 2020s is at crisis point, with England having the youngest workforce in the developed world, as reported by the OECD (2024). Having spent decades generating degree and postgraduate training and qualifications (degree to doctorate level), recent governments have removed universities as initial and continuing teacher training providers, with the inevitable decline in recruitment.

Conclusion: The Chimes

This book ends with a short vignette portraying the enthusiasm and joy of teaching and learning of a young educator who aims to commit to a lifetime of teaching. Imagine forty or more years of expertise informed by research and reflection, without multiple changes and with the engagement of university researchers alongside expert practitioners. Create a world of teachers dedicated to others.

A day wasted on others is not wasted on one's self.

Charles Dickens, *A Tale of Two Cities* (1859, p. 172)

Learn that constant change has diminished the status of the profession. How I wish that all teachers could have the opportunity to follow a master's or doctorate programme, with the time to commit to relevant studies written in the form of a dissertation or thesis. Early career teachers might then have chances and choices, which as professionals they would be able to follow as opposed to a single 'golden thread' replicated multiple times throughout their career.

Professor Sonia Blandford has spent more than 40 years in education, as teacher, school senior leader, researcher, teacher educator, university dean of education, pro-vice chancellor, school governor, MAT trustee and author; Emeritus Professor of Social Mobility Plymouth Marjon, Visiting Professor of Education UCL, Honorary Professor Warwick University; founder and former CEO of award-winning charity, Achievement for All 3As; Prince's Trust Learning Lead – Taskforce 2030; co-creator of the Teacher Training Resource Bank and Teach First programme; co-author European Commission Improving Teacher Education; founding Vice-President Chartered College of Teaching; UK lead for the European Agency for Inclusion and SEND Raising Attainment research report.

Glossary

Appropriate body (AB): An organisation responsible for ensuring that ECTs receive their statutory induction entitlement and meet the Teachers' Standards (see below) during their induction period.

Chartered College of Teaching: The professional body for teachers in England, offering resources, research and professional accreditation to support teacher development.

Coaching: A one-to-one professional development strategy where a more experienced educator supports a teacher in improving specific aspects of their practice through observation, feedback and dialogue.

Collaborative professional development: A model of CPD where teachers work together in groups or networks to share expertise, develop new skills and solve problems collectively.

Continuing professional development (CPD): The ongoing learning and training activities that teachers engage in to improve their skills, knowledge and effectiveness throughout their careers.

Core Content Framework (CCF): Sets out the minimum entitlement for trainee teachers that ITT providers and partners must draw upon when designing programmes.

Delivery partner: Organisation working with lead providers of the ECF to implement ECF programmes at a local level. They recruit schools, monitor quality and oversee mentor deployment.

Department for Education (DfE): The UK government department responsible for education policy, including teacher training and professional development.

Early Career Framework (ECF): A framework that specifies what early career teachers should learn about and practise during a two-year induction period, focusing on behaviour management, pedagogy, curriculum, assessment and professional behaviours.

Early career teacher (ECT): A teacher in their first or second year of teaching.

Early Career Teacher Entitlement (ECTE): Replacement term used by the government for the Early Career Framework (ECF) (see above) from September 2025.

Education Endowment Foundation (EEF): An independent charity dedicated to breaking the link between family income and educational achievement. The EEF supports schools, colleges and early years settings to improve teaching and learning through better use of evidence. The EEF provides advisory guidance to the DfE on the evidence base used for all teacher education and development in the 'golden thread'.

Evidence-informed practice: Teaching strategies and professional development approaches that are based on robust research evidence about what works in education.

Full induction programme: A comprehensive ECF-based training programme delivered by accredited lead providers, including mentor support and structured learning sessions.

Golden thread: The CPD pathway for teachers, from initial teacher training through to school leadership. The Early Career Framework (ECF) is considered a key component of this 'golden thread'.

Induction tutor: A role within schools responsible for overseeing the training and support provided to early career teachers (ECTs). Induction tutors coordinate registration, enrolment and assessment processes, carry out progress reviews, undertake formal assessment meetings, and ensure ECTs receive regular lesson observations and feedback.

Initial teacher training (ITT): Training undertaken by graduates to become a teacher in maintained schools across the UK, delivered by accredited ITT providers.

ITT Core Content Framework: A framework designed by the Department for Education (DfE) that sets out the minimum entitlement for all trainee teachers and the content that initial teacher training providers must include in their programmes.

Lead mentor: Experienced educator who trains and deploys mentors in schools to support the training of teachers. They receive intensive training to develop deep knowledge of the curriculum and evidence-based practices.

Mentor: A designated individual who regularly meets with the early career teacher (ECT) for structured mentoring sessions. The mentor role is to provide targeted feedback, work collaboratively to ensure the ECT receives a high-quality ECF-based induction programme, and offer subject-specific mentoring and coaching.

Mentoring: A structured relationship where an experienced teacher (mentor) supports the professional growth of a less experienced teacher (mentee), often as part of initial teacher training (ITT) or the Early Career Framework (ECF).

Multi-academy trust (MAT): A state-funded organisation, with independent regulations, that operates more than one academy school in England.

National Association of School-Based Teacher Trainers (NASBTT): Professional body for school-based ITT providers.

National Institute of Teaching (NIoT): The DfE-procured teacher education flagship organisation run by schools for schools, generating and sharing research on best practices in educator development, and offering a continuous pathway of qualifications throughout teachers' and leaders' careers, from initial teacher training to system leadership.

National professional qualifications (NPQs): A set of voluntary qualifications designed to support the professional development of experienced teachers and leaders, covering areas such as leading teacher development, behaviour and culture, teaching and literacy.

NQT (newly qualified teacher): Previously the term given to beginner teachers,

Glossary

before it changed to early career teacher (ECT) in 2021.

Ofsted: The Office for Standards in Education, Children's Services and Skills; the regulatory body responsible for inspecting and regulating services that care for children and young people, including schools and teacher training providers in England. Ofsted places emphasis on the quality of CPD as part of its inspection framework.

Pedagogy: The method and practice of teaching, encompassing both theoretical and practical aspects.

Postgraduate Certificate in Education (PGCE): An academic award that universities offer alongside qualified teacher status (QTS), available through both university-led and school-led teacher training routes.

Professional learning communities (PLCs): Groups of educators who collaborate regularly to analyse student outcomes, share practices and engage in continuous improvement.

Reflective practice: The process by which teachers critically evaluate their own teaching methods and decisions, to improve their effectiveness.

Special educational needs and disabilities (SEND): Children and young people who have learning difficulties or disabilities that make it harder for them to learn and access education in the same way as others.

Teachers' Standards (England): A set of standards outlining the minimum requirements for teachers' practice and conduct. These standards guide professional development throughout a teacher's career.

Teaching school hubs: School-led centres of excellence for professional development, playing a key role in delivering teacher training and development.

Universities' Council for the Education of Teachers (UCET): National body supporting the development of teachers and the study of education in universities.

References

Abakah, E. & Wellington, R.-M. (2023) Teacher continuous professional development (CPD) policies and practices: how do we get it right in Ghana? LinkedIn, Education in Africa, 1 June. Retrieved from www.linkedin.com/pulse/teacher-continuous-professional-development-cpd-how-do-wellington/

Allen, B., Ford, I., Hallahan, G. & Hannay, T. (2024) *Teacher Recruitment and Retention in 2024. An Exploration of Recruitment Challenges in Disadvantaged Schools*. London: Teacher Tapp, Gatsby and SchoolDash.

Allen, R. & Sims, S. (2018) Do pupils from low-income families get low-quality teachers? Indirect evidence from English schools. *Oxford Review of Education*, 44(4), 441–458.

Arhinful, E. K. (2024) Government increases continuous professional development allowance for teachers, *Joy Online*, 1 October. Retrieved from www.myjoyonline.com/government-increases-continuous-professional-development-allowance-for-teachers/

Arnold, R. & Wade, J. (2015) A definition of systems thinking: a systems approach. *Procedia Computer Science*, 44, 669–678.

Australian Government (2022) *Next Steps: Report of the Quality Initial Teacher Education Review*. Canberra: Australian Government.

Ayers, W. (1999) *Simple Justice: Thinking about Teaching and Learning, Equity and the Fight for Small Schools*. US: Education Resource Information Center. Retrieved from https://files.eric.ed.gov/fulltext/ED431829.pdf

Ball, S. J. (2003) The teacher's soul and the terrors of performativity. *Journal of Education Policy*, 18(2), 215–228.

Barrett, B. & Hordern, J. (2021) Rethinking the foundations: towards powerful professional knowledge in teacher education in the USA and England. *Journal of Curriculum Studies*, 53(2), 153–165.

Braun, V. & Clarke, V. (2022) Conceptual and design thinking for thematic analysis. *Qualitative Psychology*, 9(1), 3–26.

Bromley, M. (2024) Understanding the new Initial Teacher Training and Early Career Framework. National College news, 14 February. Retrieved from https://nationalcollege.com/news/new-initial-teacher-training

Brooks, C. (2021) The Core Content Framework and the fallacy of a teacher training 'curriculum'. IOE blog, 2 September. Retrieved from https://blogs.ucl.ac.uk/ioe/2021/09/02/the-core-content-framework-and-the-fallacy-of-a-teacher-training-curriculum/

Brooks, C. (2024) Does the new ITT and ECF hit the mark? Universities' Council for the Education of Teachers (UCET) blog, January. Retrieved from www.ucet.ac.uk/15637/the-new-ecf-and-ccf-january-2024-blog-from-professor-clare-brooks-cambridge

Buchanan, J., Prescott, A., Schuck, S., Aubusson, P., Burke, P. & Louviere, J. (2013) Teacher retention and attrition: views of early career teachers. *Australian Journal of Teacher Education*, 38(3), https://doi.org/10.14221/ajte.2013v38n3.9

Cambridge Dictionary (2022) Status. Retrieved from https://dictionary.cambridge.org/dictionary/english/status

Cambridge Dictionary (2025) Profession. Retrieved from https://dictionary.cambridge.org/dictionary/english/profession

Camera, L. (2022) Cardona: Americans shouldn't be surprised by teacher shortage, *US News*, 9 June. Retrieved from www.usnews.com/news/education-news/articles/2022-06-09/cardona-americans-shouldnt-be-surprised-by-teacher-shortage

Carter, A. (2015) *Carter Review of Initial Teacher Training (ITT)*. Retrieved from https://assets.publishing.service.gov.uk/media/5a7d63c3ed915d2d2ac08a94/Carter_Review.pdf

Chantler-Hicks, L. (2025) ECF and NPQ review: what you need to know. *Schools Week*, 10 January. Retrieved from https://schoolsweek.co.uk/ecf-and-npq-review-what-you-need-to-know/

Chartered College of Teaching (2021) Teachers still in the dark about the Early Career Framework. Chartered College of Teaching, news & events, 28 May. Retrieved from https://chartered.college/2021/05/28/teachers-still-in-the-dark-about-the-early-career-framework/

Chong, S. W., Oxley, E., Negrea, V., Bond, M., Liu, Q. & Kong, M. S. (2024) *Teacher Recruitment and Retention in Schools in Socio-economically Disadvantaged Areas in England – Review of Practice*. London: Education Endowment Foundation & National Institute of Teaching.

Church of England (2023) *Our Hope for a Flourishing Schools System: Deeply Christian, Serving the Common Good*. Church of England.

Coe, R., Aloisi, C., Higgins, S. & Major, L. E. (2014) What makes great teaching? Review of the underpinning research. Centre for Evaluation & Monitoring, Durham University & Sutton Trust. Retrieved from www.suttontrust.com/wp-content/uploads/2014/10/What-Makes-Great-Teaching-REPORT.pdf

Cohen, L., Manion, L. & Morrison, K. (2018) *Research Methods in Education*. New York: Routledge.

Cordingley, P. (2015) The contribution of research to teachers' professional learning and development. *Oxford Review of Education*, 31(2), 1–19.

Cordingley, P. & Crisp, B. (2020) Professional learning and recruitment and retention: what global regions can tell us. In T. Ovenden-Hope & R. Passy (eds), *Exploring Teacher Recruitment and Retention: Contextual Challenges from International Perspectives* (pp. 131–147). Oxon: Routledge.

Cordingley, P., Higgins, S., Greany, T., Buckler, N., Coles-Jordan, D., Crisp, B. & Coe, R. (2015) *Developing Great Teaching: Lessons from the International Reviews into Effective Professional Development*. London: Teacher Development Trust.

Creagh, S., Thompson, G., Mockler, N., Stacey, M. & Hogan, A. (2023) Workload, work intensification and time poverty for teachers and school leaders: a systematic research synthesis. *Educational Review*, 77(6), 1–20.

Cumiskey, L. (2024) New teacher training framework: everything you need to know. *Schools Week*, 30 January. Retrieved from https://schoolsweek.co.uk/dfe-combines-two-flagship-schemes-into-new-initial-teacher-training-and-early-career-framework-after-ecf-review/

Darling-Hammond, L. (2009) Recognizing and enhancing teacher effectiveness. *International Journal of Educational and Psychological Assessment*, 3, 1–24.

Darling-Hammond, L., Chung Wei, R. & Andree, A. (2010) *How High-achieving Countries Develop Great Teachers*. Stanford Center for Opportunity Policy in Education, research brief, August. Retrieved from https://edpolicy.stanford.edu/sites/default/files/publications/how-high-achieving-countries-develop-great-teachers.pdf

Darling-Hammond, L., Hyler, M. E. & Gardner, M. (2017) *Effective Teacher Professional Development*. London: Learning Policy Institute.

Davidson, S. & Camp, J. (2024) Spotlight on teacher development in Singapore. Red Kite Teaching School Hub, news & events, 5 March. Retrieved from www.redkitetsh.co.uk/spotlight-on-teacher-development-in-singapore/

Department for Education (2010) *The Importance of Teaching: The Schools White Paper 2010*. November. Retrieved from https:/assets.publishing.service.gov.uk/government/uploads/system/uploads/attachment_data/file/175429/CM-7980.pdf

Department for Education (2015) 2010 to 2015 government policy: teaching and school leadership. DfE policy paper, 8 May. Retrieved from www.gov.uk/government/publications/2010-to-2015-government-policy-teaching-and-school-leadership/2010-to-2015-government-policy-teaching-and-school-leadership

Department for Education (2018) *Strengthening Qualified Teacher Status and Improving Career Progression for Teachers. Government Consultation Response*. DfE, May. Retrieved from https://assets.publishing.service.gov.uk/media/5aec2e9ded915d42f42b627c/Government_consultation_response_-_QTS_and_career_progression.pdf

Department for Education (2019) *Teacher Retention and Recruitment Strategy*. Retrieved from https://assets.publishing.service.gov.uk/government/uploads/system/uploads/attachment_data/file/786856/DFE_Teacher_Retention_Strategy_Report.pdf

Department for Education (2019a) *Early Career Framework*, January. Retrieved from https://assets.publishing.service.gov.uk/media/60795936d3bf7f400b462d74/Early-Career_Framework_April_2021.pdf

Department for Education (2019b) School workforce in England: reporting year 2019. Retrieved from https://explore-education-statistics.service.gov.uk/find-statistics/school-workforce-in-england/2019

Department for Education (2019c) Initial Teacher Training (ITT): Core Content Framework. DfE guidance, 1 November. Retrieved from www.

gov.uk/government/publications/initial-teacher-training-itt-core-content-framework

Department for Education (2020) National professional qualifications (NPQs) reforms. DfE guidance, 3 July. Retrieved from www.gov.uk/government/publications/national-professional-qualifications-npqs-reforms/national-professional-qualifications-npqs-reforms#reformed-national-professional-qualifications

Department for Education (2021) *Initial Teacher Training (ITT) Market Review Report*. London: The Stationery Office.

Department for Education (2021a) National roll-out of the Early Career Framework. Awarded contract. DfE contract summary, 9 March. Retrieved from www.contractsfinder.service.gov.uk/Notice/53324b8e-aefc-427f-bc5b-ad65173441fe

Department for Education (2021b) New Institute of Teaching set to be established. DfE news story, 2 January. Retrieved from www.gov.uk/government/news/new-institute-of-teaching-set-to-be-established

Department for Education (2021c) *Teachers' Standards: Guidance for School Leaders, School Staff and Governing Bodies*, July. Retrieved from https://assets.publishing.service.gov.uk/government/uploads/system/uploads/attachment_data/file/1007716/Teachers__Standards_2021_update.pdf

Department for Education (2022) Changes to statutory induction for early career teachers (ECTs). DfE guidance, 3 April. Retrieved from www.gov.uk/guidance/changes-to-statutory-induction-for-early-career-teachers-ects

Department for Education (2022a) Number of early career teachers and mentors participating in the Early Career Framework. DfE transparency data, 11 March. Retrieved from www.gov.uk/government/publications/number-of-early-career-teachers-and-mentors-participating-in-the-early-career-framework

Department for Education (2022b) Opportunity for all: strong schools with great teachers for your child. DfE policy paper, 28 March. Retrieved from www.gov.uk/government/publications/opportunity-for-all-strong-schools-with-great-teachers-for-your-child

Department for Education (2022c) Delivering world-class teacher development. DfE policy paper, March. Retrieved from https://

assets.publishing.service.gov.uk/media/62850bddd3bf7f1f433ae149/ Delivering_world_class_teacher_development_policy_paper.pdf

Department for Education (2023) *Independent review of teachers' professional development in schools: phase 1 findings*. DfE/Ofsted research and analysis. Retrieved from www.gov.uk/government/publications/ teachers-professional-development-in-schools/independent-review-of-teachers-professional-development-in-schools-phase-1-findings

Department for Education (2023a) *ITT Core Content Framework and Early Career Framework: call for evidence*. DfE, 22 March. Retrieved from www.gov.uk/government/calls-for-evidence/itt-core-content-framework-and-early-career-framework-call-for-evidence

Department for Education (2024) *Emerging Findings from the NPQ Evaluation: Interim Report 2*. DfE, September. Retrieved from https:// assets.publishing.service.gov.uk/media/66e17cc5caa02d92e72c8d54/ NPQ_evaluation_interim_report_2.pdf

Department for Education (2024a) *Evaluation of the National Roll-out of the Early Career Framework Induction Programmes. Annual Summary (Year 2)*. DfE, February. Retrieved from https://assets.publishing.service. gov.uk/media/65dfa86ff1cab36b60fc475f/DfE_ECF_Report_Year2.pdf

Department for Education (2024b) *Initial Teacher Training and Early Career Framework*. DfE, January. Retrieved from https://assets.publishing. service.gov.uk/media/65b8fa60e9e10a00130310b2/Initial_teacher_training_and_early_career_framework_30_Jan_2024.pdf

Department for Education (2024c) *Induction for Early Career Teachers (England). Statutory Guidance for Appropriate Bodies, Headteachers, School Staff and Governing Bodies*. DfE, April. Retrieved from https:// assets.publishing.service.gov.uk/media/6629237f3b0122a378a7e6ef/ Induction_for_early_career_teachers__England__statutory_guidance_. pdf

Department for Education (2024d) *Outcomes of the Review of the Initial teacher Training Core Content Framework and Early Career Framework*. DfE, January. Retrieved from https://assets.publishing.service.gov.uk/ media/661d24ba08c3be25cfbd3e62/Outcomes_of_the_review_of_ the_Initial_Teacher_Training_Core_Content_Framework_and_Early_ Career_Framework.pdf

Department for Education (2024e) *The Evidence Base Underpinning the Initial Teacher Training and Early Career Framework*. Government

Response to Call for Evidence. DfE, April. Retrieved from https://assets. publishing.service.gov.uk/media/660fb22463b7f80011de18f7/The_ evidence_base_underpinning_the_Initial_Teacher_Training_and_ Early_Career_Framework_Call_for_evidence_full_response.pdf

Department for Education (2024f) *Workforce Reduction Taskforce: Initial Recommendations*. DfE, January. Retrieved from https://assets. publishing.service.gov.uk/media/65a10648e8f5ec000d1f8c2f/Workload_ reduction_taskforce_-_initial_recommendations.pdf

Department for Education (2024g) School workforce in England. DfE, 6 June. Retrieved from https://explore-education-statistics.service.gov.uk/ find-statistics/school-workforce-in-england#dataBlock-a47f5dc9-567f-4385-8bff-7e01e249884e-charts

Department for Education (2025) Managing training for early career teachers. DfE guidance, updated 10 January. Retrieved from www.gov.uk/ guidance/managing-training-for-early-career-teachers

Department for Education & Gibb, N. (2017) Nick Gibb: England's education reforms. Speech, 11 April. Retrieved from www.gov.uk/ government/speeches/nick-gibb-englands-education-reforms

Department of Education (2006) *The National Policy Framework for Teacher Education and Development in South Africa: 'More Teachers, Better Teachers'*. Retrieved from www.education.gov.za/ Portals/0/DoE%20Branches/GET/Teacher%20Education%20and%20 Development/NFTE%20Final2-HM1[1].pdf?ver=2008-03-05-111806-000

Dickens, C. (1841) *The Old Curiosity Shop*. London: Chapman & Hall.

Dickens, C. (1844) *The Chimes*. London: Chapman & Hall.

Dickens, C. (1850) *David Copperfield*. London: Bradbury & Evans.

Dickens, C. (1853) *Bleak House*. London: Bradbury & Evans.

Dickens, C. (1854) *Hard Times*. New York: Harper & Brothers.

Dickens, C. (1857) *Little Dorrit*. London: Bradbury & Evans.

Dickens, C. (1859) *A Tale of Two Cities*. London: Chapman & Hall.

Dickens, C. (1861) *Great Expectations*. London: Chapman & Hall.

Dickens, C. (1865) *Our Mutual Friend*. London: Chapman & Hall.

Dickens, C. (1898) *The Wreck of the Golden Mary*. London: Chapman & Hall.

Dickens, J. (2024) The golden thread: jewel in the crown, or tarnished tiara? *Schools Week*, 9 September. Retrieved from https://schoolsweek.co.uk/the-golden-thread-jewel-in-the-crown-or-tarnished-tiara/

Dolton, P. M., De Vries, R. & She, P.-W. (2018) *Global Teacher Status Index*. London: Varkey Foundation.

Dolton, P., McIntosh, S. & Chevalier, A. (2003) *Teacher Pay and Performance: A Review of the Literature (Bedford Way Papers, 19)*. London: Institute of Education.

Education Endowment Foundation (2021) *Effective Professional Development*. Guidance Report. London: EEF.

Education Endowment Foundation (2021a) *Evaluation of the Early Roll-out of the Early Career Framework*. National Foundation for Educational Research.

Education Policy Institute (2019) Analysis: Could phased bursaries solve the teacher retention crisis? EPI, 4 February. Retrieved from https://epi.org.uk/publications-and-research/phased-bursaries-teacher-retention/

Education Support & Public First (2023) *1970s Working Conditions in the 2020s: Modernising the Professional Lives of Teachers for the 21st Century*. Retrieved from www.educationsupport.org.uk/media/bn2bk5a3/1970s-working-conditions-in-the-2020s.pdf

Eghbal, M., Hoveida, R., Seyadat, S. A., Samavatyan, H. & Yarmohammadian, M. H. (2020) Professional development needs of teachers in rural schools. *IASE-IDJE*, 1(1), 1–15.

Ellis, V. (2024) *Teacher Education in Crisis. The State, the Market and the Universities in England*. London: Bloomsbury.

Eraut, M. (2007) Learning from other people in the workplace. *Oxford Review of Education*, 33(4), 403–422.

Eurydice (2021) Teachers in Europe: careers, development and well-being. Eurydice report, 24 March. Retrieved from https://eurydice.eacea.ec.europa.eu/sites/default/files/teachers_in_europe_2020_chapter_1.pdf

References

Eurydice (2024) Continuing professional development for teachers working in early childhood and school education. Eurydice report, 30 March. Retrieved from https://eurydice.eacea.ec.europa.eu/national-education-systems/portugal/continuing-professional-development-teachers-working-early

Evidence Based Education (2025) The great teaching toolkit. Retrieved from https://evidencebased.education/great-teaching-toolkit-cpd/

Fletcher-Wood, H. & Zuccollo, J. (2022) *The Effects of High-quality Professional Development on Teachers and Students*. EPI, Wellcome & Ambition Institute CPD review, February. Retrieved from https://epi.org.uk/wp-content/uploads/2020/02/EPI-Wellcome_CPD-Review__2020.pdf

Ford, I., Allen, B. & Wespieser, K. (2022) *Early Career Framework: One Year On*. Teacher Tapp & Gatsby. Retrieved from www.gatsby.org.uk/uploads/education/reports/pdf/2022-10-early-career-framework-tt-gatsby-final.pdf

Freedman, S. (2022) *The Gove Reforms a Decade On: What Worked, What Didn't, What Next?* Institute for Government, February. Retrieved from www.instituteforgovernment.org.uk/sites/default/files/publications/gove-reforms-decade-on.pdf

Gill, R. (2024) Why merging ITT and ECF will boost new teachers' skills. *TES Magazine*, 30 January. Retrieved from www.tes.com/magazine/analysis/general/new-teachers-qualifications-ecf-itt-framework-teacher-training

Ginnis, S., Pestell, G., Mason, E. & Knibbs, S., with Ipsos MORI (2018) *Newly Qualified Teachers: Annual Survey 2017*. Research report, September. Retrieved from https://assets.publishing.service.gov.uk/media/5b8e6cc6ed915d1eda528768/NQT_2017_survey.pdf

Greaves, E., Benfield, C. & Allen, R. (2019) Do trainee teachers harm pupil attainment? Isolating the effect of pre-service teachers on contemporaneous pupil performance in 'high-stakes' tests. *British Educational Research Journal*, 45(3), 458–482.

Grigg, R. (2015) How do we define and measure outstanding teaching? In R. Grigg, *Becoming an Outstanding Primary School Teacher*, 2nd edn (pp. 11–34). London: Routledge.

Hargreaves, L. & Flutter, J. (2013) *The Status of Teachers and the Teaching Profession: A Desk-study for Education International.* Cambridge: Department of Education, University of Cambridge.

Heeralal, P. J. (2014) Preparing pre-service teachers to teach in rural schools. *Mediterranean Journal of Social Sciences*, 5(20), 1795-1799.

HM Government (2011) *Education Act 2011.* Retrieved from www.legislation.gov.uk/ukpga/2011/21/pdfs/ukpga_20110021_en.pdf

HM Government (2012) The Education (Specified Work) (England) Regulations 2012. Retrieved from www.legislation.gov.uk/uksi/2012/762/made

Hobson, A. J., Ashby, P., Malderez, A. & Tomlinson, P. (2009) Mentoring beginning teachers: what we know and what we don't. *Teaching and Teacher Education*, 25(1), 207-216.

Hordern, J., Evans, K., Kelly, P. & Pratt, N. (2024) An expert system on flimsy foundations: teaching expertise and the Early Career Framework. *British Journal of Educational Studies*, 72(5), 607-625.

Hordern, J., Muller, J. & Deng, Z. (2021) Towards powerful educational knowledge? Addressing the challenges facing educational foundations, curriculum theory and Didaktik. *Journal of Curriculum Studies*, 53(2), 143-152.

House of Commons (2024) *Teacher Recruitment, Training and Retention. Second Report of Session 2023-4.* HC 119. London: House of Commons.

House of Commons Education Committee (2012) *Great Teachers: Attracting, Training and Retaining the Best. Ninth Report of Session 2010-12. Volume 1.* London: House of Commons.

House of Commons Education Committee (2017) *Recruitment and Retention of Teachers: Fifth Report of Session, 2016-17.* Report, together with formal minutes relating to the report. HC 199. London: House of Commons.

House of Lords (2019) *The Future of Seaside Towns. Select Committee on Regenerating Seaside Towns and Communities. Report of Session 2017-19,* HL Paper 320. Retrieved from https://publications.parliament.uk/pa/ld201719/ldselect/ldseasid

Howson, J. (2020) Shortages, what shortages? Exploring school workforce supply in England. In T. Ovenden-Hope & R. Passy (eds), *Exploring Teacher*

Recruitment and Retention: Contextual Challenges from International Perspectives (pp. 9–21). Oxon: Routledge.

Hoyle, E. (2001) Teaching: prestige, status and esteem. *Educational Management Administration & Leadership*, 29(2), 139–152.

Huling, L. & Resta, V. (2001) Teacher mentoring as professional development. *Teaching and Teacher Education*, 1–4.

Hutchings, M. (2010) *What Impact Does the Wider Economic Situation Have on Teachers' Career Decisions? A Literature Review*. London: Institute of Policy Studies, London Metropolitan University & Department for Education.

ILO/UNESCO (2016) *The ILO/UNESCO Recommendation Concerning the Status of Teachers (1966) and the UNESCO Recommendation Concerning the Status of Higher-education Teaching Personnel (1997)*. New York: Internal Labour Organization/United Nations Education, Scientific and Cultural Organization.

Ingersoll, R. M. & Gregory, G. J. (2018) The status of teaching as a profession. In J. Ballentine, J. Spade & J. Stuber (eds), *Schools and Society: A Sociological Approach to Education* (pp. 199–213). Los Angeles, CA: Sage.

Institute for Employment Studies (IES) & BMG Research (2024) *Evaluation of the National Roll-out of the Early Career Framework Induction Programmes. Annual Summary (Year 2)*. DfE, February. Retrieved from https://assets.publishing.service.gov.uk/media/65dfa86ff1cab36b60fc475f/DfE_ECF_Report_Year2.pdf

Kerney, S. (2014) Understanding beginning teacher induction: a contextualized examination of best practice. *Cogent Education*, 1(1), 967477. https://doi.org/10.1080/2331186X.2014.967477

Kime, S. (2015) 'The problem with measuring teaching quality is that there is no agreement over a definition of good teaching'. *TES Magazine*, 9 June. Retrieved from www.tes.com/magazine/archive/problem-measuring-teaching-quality-there-no-agreement-over-definition-good

Kraft, M. P. (2014) Can professional environments in schools promote teacher development? Explaining heterogeneity in returns to teaching experience. *Educational Evaluation and Policy Analysis*, 36(4), 476–500.

Kvale, S. (1996) *Interviews*. London: Sage.

Lee, C. (2025) Teacher professionalism: concepts, definitions, opportunities. From the Editor. *Impact*, 1–4.

Lindorff, A., Jentsch, A., Walkington, C., Kaiser, G. & Sammons, P. (2020) Hybrid content-specific and generic approaches to lesson observation: possibilities and practicalities. *Studies in Educational Evaluation*, 67(67). https://doi.org/10.1016/j.stueduc.2020.100919

Long, R. & Danechi, S. (2021) Teacher recruitment and retention in England. House of Commons Briefing Paper.

Luo, Y., Guo, F. & Shi, J. (2022) Professional development needs and challenges of rural teachers in China: a systematic review. *Teaching and Teacher Education*, 110, 103572.

Madgwick, H. (2020) Do years in the profession make you a better teacher? EEF blog, 8 September. Retrieved from https://educationendowmentfoundation.org.uk/news/eef-blog-do-years-in-the-profession-make-you-a-better-teacher

Madgwick, H. (2024) The updated Core Content and Early Career Framework: what's changed? EEF blog, 31 January. Retrieved from https://educationendowmentfoundation.org.uk/news/the-updated-core-content-and-early-career-framework-whats-changed

Maisuria, A., Long, R. & Danechi, S. (2023) *Teacher Recruitment and Retention in England*. London: House of Commons Library.

Martin, M. (2024) Early career and trainee teachers to share updated framework. *TES Magazine*, 30 January. Retrieved from www.tes.com/magazine/news/general/early-career-teachers-itt-teacher-training-updated-framework

McClean, D., Worth, J. & Smith, A. (2024) *Teacher Labour Market in England. Annual Report 2024*. NFER, March. Retrieved from www.nfer.ac.uk/media/hqdglvra/teacher_labour_market_in_england_annual_report_2024.pdf

McIntyre, J., Youens, B. & Stevenson, H. (2017) Silenced voices: the disappearance of the university and the student teacher in teacher education policy discourse in England. *Research Papers in Education*, 34(3), 1–15.

Menzies, L. (2019) The DfE's recruitment and retention strategy: the good the bad and the ugly … . Centre for Education and Youth blog, 28

January. Retrieved from https://cfey.org/2019/01/the-dfes-recruitment-and-retention-strategy-the-good-the-bad-and-the-ugly/

Menzies, L. & Quilter-Pinner, H. (2023) Improvement through empowerment: helping our teachers and schools be the best they can be. IPPR, 21 November. Retrieved from www.ippr.org/articles/improvement-through-empowerment

Muijs, D. & Reynolds, D. (2018) Introduction: effective teaching – the British research reviewed. In D. Muijs & D. Reynolds, *Effective Teaching: Evidence and Practice*, 4th edn (pp. 1–12). London: Sage.

Murtagh, L., Dawes, L., Rushton, E. & Ball-Smith, C. (2024) Early career teacher mentoring in England: a case study of compliance and mediation. *Professional Development in Education*, published online 19 January. https://doi.org/10.1080/19415257.2023.2291357

Mutton, T., Burn, K. & Menter, I. (2017) Deconstructing the Carter Review: competing conceptions of quality in England's 'school-led' system of initial teacher education. *Journal of Education Policy*, 32(1), 14–33.

NASUWT (2019) *Big Question Survey – Explore the Data*. Retrieved from www.nasuwt.org.uk/be-involved/big-question-survey/big-question-survey-explore-the-data.html

NASUWT (2021) Early Career Framework (England). Retrieved from www.nasuwt.org.uk/advice/in-the-classroom/professionalism/teacher-training-professionalism-england-/early-career-framework-england.html#Terminology

National Association of Head Teachers (2021) *How Has the Early Career Framework Landed in Schools?* Retrieved from www.naht.org.uk/Portals/0/PDF's/NAHT%20ECF%20Survey%20FINAL%20Pub.pdf?ver=2021-12-16-201611-260

Niemtus, Z. (2024) What can Singapore teach us about education in England? *TES Magazine*, 18 December. Retrieved from www.tes.com/magazine/teaching-learning/general/what-singapore-can-teach-us-about-education-in-england

OECD (2014) *TALIS 2013 Results: An International Perspective on Teaching and Learning*. Paris: OECD Publishing.

OECD (2024) *Education Policy Outlook 2024: Reshaping Teaching into a Thriving Profession from ABCs to AI*. Paris: OECD Publishing. Retrieved from https://doi.org/10.1787/dd5140e4-en

Ofsted (2019) Education inspection framework No. 190015. Retrieved from https://feweek.co.uk/wp-content/uploads/2019/05/Education_inspection_framework.pdf

Ofsted (2021) Terms of reference: Ofsted's independent review of teachers' professional development. Research and analysis, 22 September. Retrieved from www.gov.uk/government/publications/ofsteds-independent-review-of-teachers-professional-development/terms-of-reference-ofsteds-independent-review-of-teachers-professional-development

Ovenden-Hope, T., Passy, R. & Iglehart, P. (2022) Educational isolation and the challenge of 'place' for securing a high-quality teacher supply. In I. Menter (ed.), *The Palgrave Handbook of Teacher Education Research* (pp. 1–22). London: Palgrave Macmillan.

Ovenden-Hope, T. (2021) Teacher as commodity versus teacher as professional: an international status-based crisis in teacher supply. *Impact*, 11, 71–74.

Ovenden-Hope, T. (2022) *The Early Career Framework: Origins, Outcomes and Opportunities*. Woodbridge: John Catt.

Ovenden-Hope, T. (2022a) A status-based crisis of teacher shortages? Exploring the role of 'status' in teacher recruitment and retention. *Research in Teacher Education*, 12(1), 36–42.

Ovenden-Hope, T. (2022b) Afterword. In T. Ovenden-Hope (ed.), *The Early Career Framework: Origins, Outcomes and Opportunities* (pp. 293–303). Woodbridge: John Catt.

Ovenden-Hope, T. (2023) Opinion: MPs are right – teacher recruitment and retention are in crisis. *Marjon News*, 11 November. Retrieved from www.marjon.ac.uk/about-marjon/news-and-events/marjon-news/opinion-mps-are-right---teacher-recruitment-and-retention-are-in-crisis.html

Ovenden-Hope, T. (2024) An evaluation of education policy in England since 2010 and the policy consequences for small primary schools. *Education Sciences*, 14(11), 1164.

Ovenden-Hope, T. (2024a) Editorial. *Impact*, 22, Autumn, 1–4. Retrieved from https://my.chartered.college/impact_article/from-the-editor-9/

Ovenden-Hope, T. & Kirkpatrick, H. (2024) The Early Career Framework: why context matters for teacher professional development. *Education Sciences*, 14(11), 1261. https://doi.org/10.3390/educsci14111261

References

Ovenden-Hope, T. & Kirkpatrick, H. (2025) Exploring education policy and reform in England (2010–2024) and the Early Career Framework: the unfolding of an education 'market' for teacher development. In R. Morris & T. Perry (eds), *Education Policy 2010–2024*. London: Taylor & Francis.

Ovenden-Hope, T. & Passy, R. (2019) Educational isolation: a challenge for schools in England. Retrieved from www.marjon.ac.uk/educational-isolation/

Ovenden-Hope, T. & Passy, R. (2020) *Exploring Teacher Recruitment and Retention: Contextual Challenges from International Perspectives*. Oxon: Routledge.

Ovenden-Hope, T., Blandford, S., Cain, T. & Maxwell, B. (2018) RETAIN early career teacher retention programme: evaluating the role of research informed continuing professional development for a high quality, sustainable 21st century teaching profession. *Journal of Education for Teaching*, 44(5), 590–607.

Ovenden-Hope, T., Blandford, S., Cain, T. & Maxwell, B. (2020) RETAIN: a research-informed model of continuing professional development for early career teacher retention. In T. Ovenden-Hope & R. Passy (eds) *Exploring Recruitment and Retention: Contextual Challenges from International Perspectives* (pp. 59–72). Oxon: Routledge.

Plymouth Marjon University (2021) What is the Early Career Framework? Retrieved from www.marjon.ac.uk/how-to-get-into-teaching/what-is-the-early-career-framework/

Podolsky, A., Kini, T. & Darling-Hammond, L. (2019) Does teaching experience increase teacher effectiveness? A review of US research. *Journal of Professional Capital and Community*, 4(4), 286–308.

Qing, G., Eleftheriadou, S. & Baines, L. (2023) *The Impact of the Early Career Framework Programme on the Work Engagement, Wellbeing and Retention of Teachers: A Longitudinal Study, 2021–2026. Interim Research Report 2*. UCL.

Roberts, J. & Nordern, J. (2024) Four providers awarded contracts to deliver the ECF. *TES Magazine*, 21 November. Retrieved from www.tes.com/magazine/news/general/four-providers-awarded-contracts-deliver-ecf

Rowe, J. (2024) A 'golden thread'? Teacher recruitment, retention and the market review in England. In V. Ellis (ed.), *Teacher Education in Crisis. The State, the Market and the Universities in England*. London: Bloomsbury.

Secretary of State for Education (2022) *Opportunity for All: Strong Schools with Great Teachers for Your Child*. HM Government white paper, March. Retrieved from https://assets.publishing.service.gov.uk/government/uploads/system/uploads/attachment_data/file/1063602/Opportunity_for_all_strong_schools_with_great_teachers_for_your_child__print_version_.pdf

Secretary of State for Housing, Communities and Local Government (2018) *Building a Safer Future. Independent Review of Building Regulations and Fire Safety: Final Report*, May. Retrieved from https://assets.publishing.service.gov.uk/media/5afc50c840f0b622e4844ab4/Building_a_Safer_Future_-_web.pdf

See, B. H. (2022) Where have we gone wrong in our battle against teacher shortages? *Open Access News*, 5 October. Retrieved from www.openaccessgovernment.org/where-have-we-gone-wrong-in-our-battle-against-teacher-shortages/140272/

See, B., Gorard, S., Morris, R. & El Soufi, N. (2020) How to recruit and retain teachers in hard-to-staff areas: a systematic review of the empirical evidence. In T. Ovenden-Hope & R. Passy (eds), *Exploring Teacher Recruitment and Retention: Contextual Challenges from International Perspectives* (pp. 148–163). London: Routledge.

See, B., Morris, R., Gorard, S., Kokotsaki, D. & Abdi, S. (2020) What works in attracting and retaining teachers in challenging schools and areas? *Oxford Review of Education*, 46(6), 678–697.

Simpson, T., Hastings, W. & Hill, B. (2007) 'I knew that she was watching me': the professional benefits of mentoring. *Teachers and Teaching*, 13(5), 481–498.

Sims, S., Fletcher-Wood, H., O'Mara-Eves, A., Cottingham, S., Stansfield, C., Van Herwegen, J. & Anders, J. (2021) What are the characteristics of effective teacher professional development? A systematic review & meta-analysis. Education Endowment Foundation report, October. Retrieved from https://d2tic4wvo1iusb.cloudfront.net/production/documents/pages/Teacher-professional-development.pdf?v=1742813168

Skourdoumbis, A. (2017) Assessing the productivity of schools through two 'what works' inputs, teacher quality and teacher effectiveness. *Educational Research for Policy and Practice*, 16(3), 205–217.

Stacey, R. (1996) *Complexity and Creativity in Organizations*. San Francisco, CA: Berrett-Koehler Publications.

Steadman, S. & Ellis, V. (2021) Teaching quality, social mobility and 'opportunity' in England: the case of the teaching and leadership innovation fund. *European Journal of Teacher Education*, 44(3), 399–414. https://doi.org/10.1080/02619768.2021.1901078

Stewart, V. (2018) How teachers around the world learn. ASCD *Educational Leadership Magazine*, 76(3), 1 November.

Sutton Trust (2011) Improving the impact of teachers on pupil achievement in the UK – interim findings. Sutton Trust report, 21 September. Retrieved from www.suttontrust.com/our-research/improving-impact-teachers-pupil-achievement-uk-interim-findings

Thomas, L., Tuytens, M., Moolenaar, N., Devos, G., Kelchtermans, G. & Vanderlinde, R. (2019) Teachers' first year in the profession: the power of high-quality support. *Teachers and Teaching*, 25(2), 160–188.

Turvey, K. (2024) England's essentialist teacher education policy frameworks as double texts. In V. Ellis (ed.), *Teacher Education in Crisis. The State, the Market and Universities in England* (pp. 117–132). London: Bloomsbury.

Tzivinikou, S. (2015) The impact of an in-service training program on the self-efficacy of special and general education teachers. *Problems of Education in the 21st Century*, 64(1), 95–107.

UNESCO (2015) *SDG4 – Education 2030. Framework for Action*. Paris: UNESCO.

Universities UK (2014) *The Impact of Initial Teacher Training Reforms on English Higher Education Institutions*. Retrieved from https://dera.ioe.ac.uk/id/eprint/26200/1/ImpactOfITTreformsOnEnglishHEIs.pdf

Universities' Council for the Education of Teachers (2019) *Overview of the Recruitment and Retention Strategy and Early Career Framework*. UCET.

Universities' Council for the Education of Teachers (2022) *Golden Thread or Gilded Cage? An Analysis of Department for Education Support for the Continuing Professional Development of Teachers*. UCET, November.

Retrieved from www.ucet.ac.uk/downloads/14605-Gilded-Cage-UCET-CPD-position-paper-%28full-version%29.pdf

Uttley, S. (2021) *Early Career Framework: School Leaders' Early Experiences of the New Model*. Koinonia Group research paper 1/22.

Van den Brande, J. & Zuccollo, J. (2021) *The Cost of High-quality Professional Development for Teachers in England*. Wellcome & Education Policy Institute report, July. Retrieved from https://epi.org.uk/wp-content/uploads/2021/07/2021-Cost-of-quality-teacher-cpd_EPI.pdf

Walters, D. (2022) Commentary: Covid-19 school closures undermined learning. *CalMatters*, 18 September. Retrieved from https://calmatters.org/commentary/2022/09/covid-19-school-closures-undermined-learning

Worth, J. & Faulkner, E. (2022) *Teacher Labour Market in England: Annual Report*. Slough: NFER.

Worth, J. & Van den Brande, J. (2020) *Teacher Autonomy: How Does It Relate to Job Satisfaction and Retention?* NFER. Retrieved from https://tdtrust.org/wp-content/uploads/2020/08/teacher_autonomy_how_does_it_relate_to_job_satisfaction_and_retention-1.pdf

Worth, J., Lynch, S., Hillary, J., Rennie, C. & Andrade, J. (2018) Teacher Workforce Dynamics in England: Nurturing, Supporting and Valuing Teachers. NFER report, October. Retrieved from www.nfer.ac.uk/media/lstdnhdh/teacher_workforce_dynamics_in_england_final_report.pdf

Index

Accountability 2, 9, 49, 114
Adaptive teaching 58, 103, 115
Agency (teacher) 3, 116
Assessment 43, 56, 123
Attrition (teacher) 2, 6, 25, 71
Professional development 3, 120–124
Chartered College of Teaching 18, 73, 140
Classroom management 44, 56
Cognitive science 20, 49, 114
Contextualisation (of training) 3, 48, 67, 83, 103
Continued Professional Development (CPD) 3, 120, 123
Core Content Framework (CCF) 2, 20, 55, 58, 100–105
Diversity, Equity, Inclusion (DEI) 115
Early Career Framework (ECF) 2, 18, 31, 56, 67–98
Early Career Teacher Entitlement (ECTE) 3, 98, 114
Education Endowment Foundation (EEF) 20, 43, 114
Educational isolation 121
Evidence-informed practice 20, 43, 114
Feedback (teacher) 45, 123
Frameworks (teacher development) 2, 41–61, 99–117

Golden thread (of teacher development) 2, 22, 30, 114
Great teachers 2, 41–61
Induction tutor 87–93
Initial Teacher Training (ITT) 2, 20, 55, 99–117
ITTECF (Initial Teacher Training and Early Career Framework) 2, 58, 99–117
Mentoring 2, 68–86, 103–109,115
National Professional Qualifications (NPQs) 2, 57, 114
Pedagogy 2, 43, 114
Place-based equity 121
Professional development 3, 120–124
Professional learning communities (PLCs) 113, 123
Qualified Teacher Status (QTS) 10, 55
Recruitment (teacher) 1, 5, 25
Retention (teacher) 1, 6, 25, 120
Self-efficacy (teacher) 2, 70, 120
SEND (Special Educational Needs and Disabilities) 58, 103, 115
Status (of teaching) 9, 10, 13
Teacher experience case studies 8, 17, 51, 93, 106
Teaching quality 43, 49